A touch of

MONACO
AND THE FRENCH
RIVIERA GUIDE

a selective guide in plain English

Publisher:	Mary Stuart Gordon
Editor:	David Ward-Perkins
Cover, Sketches:	Sempé
Photographs:	William McNabb, Jr.
Editorial Assistants:	Jill Harry, Mary Deschamps, MacLowe
Maps:	Mark Batkin
Layout:	Josette Theilot
Contributing Editors:	Roger Collins, Gary Crowfoot, June Freeman, Mavis Guinard, Jill Harry, Brandy Kail, Roger Laing, Joanne McNabb, Joel Stratt-McClure

Photographic Credits: Courtesy of La Société des Bains de Mer (p.130); Courtesy of Janet Greenberg & Max Agostini (pp.156-157). All other photos by William McNabb, Jr., featuring Jazz Musician, Toots Thielmans (pp. 154-155) and Chef Maximen of the **Chantecler**, Nice (p.149).

Distribution

France:
Les Editions de Virginie
36, rue du Colisée
PARIS 75008
Tel: 42.89.49.99
Telex: 643 739 TRADTOP

UK:
Roger Lascelles
Lascelles Ltd.
47, York Road
Brentford, Middlesex
TW 80QP UK
Tel: (01) 847-0935

USA:
European Publishers
Representatives
Charles Treves
11-03 46th Avenue
Long Island City, NY 11101
Tel: (718) 937-4606
Telex: 620 974 HACH

Bookpeople
Randall Beek
2929 Fifth Street
Berkeley, CA 94710
Tel: (415) 549-3030

We wish to gratefully acknowledge our thanks to the following for their contributions to this guide: Nabil Boustany, Côte d'Azur Developpement, Philippe Cywan, Philippe Lorin, MacLowe, La Société des Bains de Mer, Hélène Starozum.

The Touch Guides are Traders & Travelers Ltd. publications (8 Victoria Street, Douglas, Isle of Man, Registration n° 27098). Traders & Travelers is represented in France by **Les Editons de Virginie**, 36, rue du Colisée, 75008 Paris. Tel: (1) 42.89.49.99. and **Joanne McNabb**, 7, rue de la Pourtoune, Saint-Paul-de Vence 06570 Tel: 93.32..61.18 and in Switzerland by **Roy Kietzman**, rue Rothschild 68, 1202 Geneva, Switzerland. Tel: (022) 32.08.79. and in the United States by **European Publishers Representatives** (see address above).

ISBN: 2-9500956-2-3

Table of Contents

1. The Dream Is Still Real: Getting the Best Out of the Riviera 7
David Ward-Perkins
Gary Crowfoot

2. Monaco: The Glamour and the Gold 29
June Freeman

The grand Excursion: The Roads 53
Roger Collis

3. Nice: The Suntanned Queen of the Rivera 59
David Ward-Perkins,
Jill Harry

4. The Heart of the Riviera: Antibes, Juan-les-Pins, Cagnes-sur-Mer, Vence and Saint Paul 83
David Ward-Perkins

5. The Festival City: Cannes and the Cannois Region 103
Joanne NcNabb

6. Saint-Tropez: The Stars and the Sea 119
Mavis Guinard

7. Eating Out on the Riviera: A Taste of a Great Art 171
David Ward-Perkins

8. Riviera Nightlife 185
Roger Laing

9. The Sporting Life 203
Joel Stratte-McClure

The Verdon: A New Sports Area 212
Mavis Guinard

10. Bringing the Kids Along Too 217
Brandy Kail

11. Doing Business on the Riviera 231
Joel Stratte-McClure

A touch of
MONACO
AND THE FRENCH
RIVIERA
GUIDE
a selective guide in plain English

— « *Heureusement, il me reste le rêve...* »

1
THE DREAM IS STILL REAL: GETTING THE BEST OUT OF THE RIVIERA

8 | A Brief Introduction
10 | Using the "Touch"
11 | Getting Started
12 | Climate
12 | Arriving By Air
16 | Trains
17 | Buses
17 | Taxis
17 | Banks & Money
19 | Shopping
20 | Cafés & Restaurants
21 | Tourism
21 | Activities & Culture
22 | Magazines/Newspapers/Books
23 | Hairdressers
23 | Pharmacies/Chemists
24 | Emergencies
24 | Consulates
24 | Lost and Found
25 | Telephone
25 | Post Offices
26 | Religious Services
27 | TV/Radio
27 | Hotels

The visitor to Monaco and the French Riviera comes with many preconceived notions. The mythology of the Riviera includes casinos and palm-trees, beaches and night-clubs, bikinis and evening-dress. It is the land of Bardot and Vadim, but also of a host of international stars, of writers and artists, of princes, countesses and lords. On the Riviera, so the legend goes, everyone is famous, suntanned and rich. Stunning blondes pull their Porsches up to the Grand Hotel, and throw the keys to the liveried doorman. Waiting photographers admire the flawless diamonds that set off their sun-browned complexions and wind-swept hair. Just in time to change into the Dior with the plunging neckline, before heading for the *première* of the latest film at the *Palais des Festivals* .

The first shock on arrival is to find that the Riviera exists: it isn't just a dream. Several million people actually live here: working, bringing up children and going about other unromantic activities. There are cities, housing-estates and even slums. There is traffic, and queues, and pickpockets and trains that run late. There are parts of the coast that are as crowded as any major metropolis. And yet...

And yet, the Riviera *is* special. Although greater Nice is swallowing up the surrounding villages, the result, in ten years time, will be one of the most beautiful cities in the world. At Sophia Antipolis, they are building a vast technology-park, where it's hard to see the buildings for the trees. In fact, on the IBM site at La Gaude, the new buildings are all *underground* , so as not to stand out.

Zoning laws also protect the medieval villages, where a new generation of artisans and craftspeople are moving in to rebuild, and to revive traditions. In every town along the coast, there are new conference centres, concert halls and sports facilities, most of them tastefully designed to fit into the landscape. After decades as the playground of other regions and nations, the Riviera is building and developing on its own.

The playground, of course, is still very active, and magnificent blondes in their Porsches can rest assured — their days are not numbered. It is unlikely that any city in the world can boast more millionaires per square foot than Cannes (unless it's Monaco). The flowers and palm-trees of the Croisette, in front of the glistening white Hotels Carlton and Martinez still take your breath away for sheer style. The purr of Rolls-Royces, and the clicking of pappa-razzis' lenses can still be heard from the beaches, blending with the harmonious tinkle of expensive jewelry.

In Monte Carlo, the atmosphere of discreet luxury is such that you hesitate to raise your voice, even in the street. In Saint-Tropez on the other hand, the world is a stage to strut and display on, and if you *lower* your voice, you won't be heard above the fashionable buzz. In these same streets, nakedness is worn with the same panache and elegance as designer clothes. Without self-consciousness, or prudery, because this is the land that invented tolerance and good living.

Good living is as natural to the Riviera as sunshine and the mild climate. And the pleasures aren't limited to millionaires. Within the budget of the average traveller, there are hundreds of superb restaurants. There are cafés and bars to while away lazy hours, in the heart of graceful towns and picturesque villages. There are nightspots to keep you busy till the early hours, and elegant hotels where you can sleep off the effects.

All this against the backdrop of the snow-covered Alps, with green forests and hills in the foreground, and the blue Mediterranean at your feet. On perfect days, with a light breeze ruffling the palm-trees, driving past beautiful villas on the way to the beach, the sense of unreality takes over again. Can this really be true? Or is it just a Hollywood dream, a stage-set for stars and princes, that will vanish when you awake?

Riviera or Côte d'Azur: A Little Semantics

The French Riviera runs from the Italian frontier westward, via Monaco, Nice and Cannes to the rocky outcrop of the Esterel. The name was given in the 19th century by the English aristocrats who spent the winter months in Nice, far from the snow and ice of their home country. More recently, the French have christened the same region the "Côte d'Azur" (and added the region of Saint-Tropez). Typically, the French and English have insisted on maintaining their own name, and both "Riviera" and "Côte d'Azur" are now commonly used.

Equally typically, nobody consulted the original inhabitants of this region. Not that they would have cared. The populations of the Riviera have accepted their colonisation by tourists with characteristic unconcern. Having already been overrun by Greeks, Romans, Arabs and Italians, to name but a few, they take this new invasion very calmly. It's a more welcome invasion than many, because made in the name of elegance, leisure and *joie de vivre* .

One final complication, to add to the semantic muddle, is that Monaco (and Monte Carlo), while part of the Riviera, are certainly not part of the *French* Riviera, since Monaco is a sovereign state, independent from France.

There is also the *Italian* Riviera. But that's another story....

USING THE "TOUCH"

A Touch of Monaco and the French Riviera (in the same series as *A Touch of Paris* and *A Touch of Geneva*) was written by a group of writers and journalists, all of whom live there and love the region dearly. To compile the guide, they shared their experiences and those of their friends. They consulted with experts, and went out in the field to check what they had heard. Then each one wrote about what he or she knew best, the things they appreciated and felt were exceptional.

The instructions they got from the editors were simple, "Recommend what you would recommend to your own friends on a visit." We have made a considerable effort to eliminate the indifferent and the obvious. The guide is an indication of what is *really* marvellous (not just touristy), and a source of information unavailable elsewhere.

The Riviera is a series of towns or areas, stretching along the coast. This guide follows these towns in a North-East to

South-Westerly direction (starting with Monaco and ending with Saint-Tropez), with recommended excursions to other towns and villages within each chapter.

Some questions do not fit this format easily. For example, a visitor would probably prefer to have all the casinos listed together. For that reason, **Nightlife** has a chapter of its own. Other subjects treated separately are **Eating Out**, **Sports**, doing **Business**, and what to do with **Children**.

Unlike other *Touch* guides, this one deals with an entire region. Therefore, the information found in this chapter, *touches* on practical information in a very general manner leaving most of the detailed information to specific chapters.

No system is perfect, but we don't think it's difficult to find your way through this book. It is, in any case, a *touch* of Monaco and the French Riviera, something to dip into and discover, something to make your stay a pleasure and an adventure.

David Ward-Perkins

DAVID WARD-PERKINS is a freelance writer and journalist working on the French Riviera. His special fields are high-tech business, education and tourism.

GETTING STARTED

The thing to remember about life on the Riviera is that everything takes a little longer to do than you expect. The French use an Italian word to describe this Mediterranean attitude, *farniente*, the art of putting off till next week what you could do tomorrow. Our advice to you is to go native and take life as it comes. Relax. Slow down. Maybe we don't do things as efficiently here as in London or New York, but then didn't you come here to get away from those places?

CLIMATE

Everyone thinks of the Riviera as being blessed with eternal blue skies and mild temperatures. Most of the time it is. However, there are times when it can be frankly cold and wet — it even snowed heavily in Nice and Cannes in the winters of '85 and '86.

In fact, it rains more in Nice (34" per year) than in the north of France (24"), but the rain falls on only 60 days (compared with 171 days in the north). This means you can count on 300 days of sunshine per year: and local people are shocked if it rains for more than 24 hours!

From early June to the end of September you are usually assured sunshine. July and August are HOT. December and January are often sunny because of the Mistral: a cold dry wind that brings dazzling blue skies and incredible visibility (you may even see Corsica if you get up at the crack of dawn).

The average temperature ranges from 9°C (Jan/Feb) to 23°C (July).

However, there are significant local variations in climate. With mountains of 10,000 feet only 50 miles from the sea, you can choose between skiing and sunbathing on the beach at certain times of the year.

Weather Information by Phone (in French)
Land: 93.83.91.11
Sea: 93.83.91.12
Mountains: 93.71.01.21

ARRIVING BY AIR

You'll arrive at **Nice-Cote d'Azur International Airport** — an exciting landing because the runways have been extended and you have the impression of landing on the sea. Palm trees and the warm Mediterranean air immediately bring smiles of pleasure to even the most weary of travelers.

There are 15 flights daily between Nice and Paris and connections to 50 major foreign cities and 22 French towns

sempé

The airport is on a *human scale* and you'll find people friendly and helpful, even if you don't speak French. The facilities include all major car-rental agencies; banking and foreign-exchange facilities; a helicopter service for Monaco (Tel: 93.21.34.62 and see below); shops; duty-free (outgoing flights only); international newspaper shop, etc.

For getting to your hotel/villa, you have the choice between:

— **TAXI** service (***approximately*** 100 F to Nice; 280 F + plus motorway toll to Cannes; 350 F to Monaco).

— **HELICOPTER** service to Monaco costs 270 F (500 F during the Grand Prix period) and takes only 10 minutes.

— **EXPRESS MINI-BUS** (**STANCA**) to Nice, Antibes, Cannes, Monaco and Sophia Antipolis; tickets are on sale inside the airport.

DRIVING

The **A7** motorway (a toll road) is part of a continuous connection between the north of Europe and the South of Italy. Exit at the appropriate interchange. If you come here from Paris, you'll pass next to towns like Dijon, Lyon, Montélimar, Avignon, Aix — all tempting and worth the detour. If you want to eat well, it's best to leave the motorway and go into the centre of one of the towns. Remember that the speed limit on motorways is **130 km/h**, and speeding tickets are quite frequent and expensive in holiday periods.

Drive defensively! You'll find that cars pass you on the right and on the left and that maximum speed limits are often taken to mean minimum speed by local drivers. The *Promenade des Anglais* on Friday and Saturday evenings resembles a slalom course.

Drivers here express themselves liberally with hooters, lights, voice and gestures. Don't take it too seriously. Note that cars coming from the right generally have right-of-way, even if you are on the main road. Be careful, because local drivers take full advantage of this aspect of the French highway code.

In the holiday season a lot of drivers are here for the first time — they're not sure where they're going and they may be looking at the scenery rather than the car in front of them. And remember that narrow mountain roads bring out the Monte-Carlo Rally spirit in the most placid of motorists.

Tourists only need a valid driving license issued in their own country; however, it's a good idea get an international driving license, just in case.

CAR RENTAL

You can rent cars easily at the airport or at agencies in all major towns. All major companies are represented on the *Côte*.

Hertz

MONACO

57, rue Grimaldi

Tel: 93.50.79.60

NICE
Airport
Tel: 93.21.36.72

SAINT-TROPEZ
Rue de la Nouvelle Poste
Tel: 94.97.22.01

Avis

MONACO
9, avenue Astende
Tel: 93.30.17.53

NICE
Airport
Tel: 93.212.36.33

SAINT-TROPEZ
13, boulevard Louis Blanc
Tel: 94.97.03.10

Europcar

MONACO
47, avenue Grande Bretagne
Tel: 93.50.74.95

NICE
Airport
Tel: 93.21.36.44

SAINT-TROPEZ
Quai de l'Epi
Tel: 94.97.15.41

24 HOUR BREAKDOWN SERVICE

If you break down on the motorway, there are emergency phones at regular intervals where you can call for assistance. The fixed fee (approximately 260 F) is marked on the phone booth. Other local breakdown services:

ANTIBES
Tel: 93.61.09.09

CANNES
Tel: 93.39.23.74

MONACO
Beausoleil
Tel: 93.78.8.68

NICE
Tel: 93.88.67.17

SAINT-TROPEZ
Cougolin
Tel: 94.93.25.52

TRAINS

Generally speaking, train stations are found in the center of the town and taxis are available outside the station. There are also foreign exchange facilities in Nice and Cannes stations. The coastal towns are well-served by the **SNCF** (railway), and the train is a fast and inexpensive way of getting along the coast, particularly in summer when traffic jams abound. Be sure to punch your ticket in the special machines at the entrance to the platform before getting on the train, otherwise you could be in for a fine.

SNCF INFORMATION

NICE
Tel: 93.87.50.50

CANNES
Tel: 93.99.50.50

MONACO
Tel: 93.30.25.53

BUSES

There is a network of buses serving all the region and they are a good way to visit the inland areas (*arrière pays*) if you want to avoid driving. However, buses are not especially frequent, and you are advised to check schedules carefully before leaving and make double sure that you have taken into account changes for public holidays and Sundays. Timetable information can be obtained at the main bus station (*Gare routière*) in Nice or Cannes. In Monaco, buses stop in front of the train station.

CANNES
Place de l'Hôtel de Ville
Tel: 93.39.54.40

NICE
Gare Routière
Tel: 93.85.61.81

TAXIS

A convenient but rather expensive way of getting around, especially if you cross the boundary to the town-centre zone. To order a taxi, call:

CANNES
Railway Station
Tel: 93.38.30.79

NICE
Taxis Ville de Nice
Tel: 93.82.32.32

SAINT-TROPEZ
Taxi, Saint-Tropez
Tel: 94.97.40.86

BANKS & MONEY

In general, you'll find the service in banks is pretty slow and not always with a smile. However, there is usually somebody who speaks sufficient English to deal with most everyday transactions. Many banks, though not all, have foreign exchange facilities.

Bank opening hours can vary from one bank to another, but are usually Monday to Friday 8:30-11:45 am and 1:45-4:30 pm. The foreign-exchange desk sometimes closes even earlier. Check times at the local branch in advance to be sure.

Note that banks close on public holidays and frequently close in the case of a *pont* — a long weekend which stretches to include public holidays falling on a Tuesday or Thursday.

You can use credit cards, Eurocheques or travellers checks in most shops, hotels and restaurants. **VISA** is the most commonly accepted credit card; **American Express** in the more expensive places. Cash dispensers accepting a variety of credit cards exist ouside most ban

EXCHANGE FACILITIES

OPEN SUNDAYS AND/OR PUBLIC HOLIDAYS

THOMAS COOK
Train station
NICE
Tel: 93.88.15.84

AIRPORT EXCHANGE
NICE
Tel: 93.72.30.30

CASINO EXCHANGE
Casino
MONACO
Tel: 93.30.00.39

BANKS

American Express

CANNES
3, La Croisette
Tel: 93.39.84.67

MONACO
5, rue de Monte Carlo Tel:
93.50.07.77

NICE
2, rue Congrès
Tel: 93.87.11.76

Barclays

CANNES
63, boulevard Maréchal Juin
Tel: 93.20.97.42

MONACO
31, avenue de la Costa
Tel: 93.50.67.11

NICE
2, rue Alphonse Karr
Tel: 93.87.92.31

SHOPPING

If you enjoy shopping, the Riviera is a delight. Both Cannes and Nice have the full range of *name* shops, centered on **rue d'Antibes** in Cannes and on the pedestrian zone next to **Place Massena** in Nice. However, you'll find interesting and original shops in the streets around these areas, so don't hesitate to explore. **Juan-les-Pins** offers the latest in the season's fashion and perhaps the best selection of clothes for being well-dressed and almost undressed on the beach.

Shopping Hours

Large stores and supermarkets rarely open before 10 am and stay open until 7 pm; late-night shopping usually means Friday until 8 pm. Most shops close for lunch, from noon to 2 or 3 pm. On Sundays, you can't buy much more than a loaf of bread and the newspaper, although you may find street markets and corner grocery stores open until noon. Monday is closing day for hairdressers in particular.

Shopping Centers

Cap 3000, at St. Laurent du Var (between Nice and Cannes) — dozens of boutiques plus a department store and a supermarket that stocks some English/American food items.

Nice Etoile, Av. Jean Medecin, Nice — everything from records to shoes plus an art-gallery on the top floor.

Galeries Lafayette, Place Massena, Nice — the largest department store in Nice.

Markets

For local colour and an astonishing array of flowers, fruit, cheeses and vegetables, the markets are unbeatable. On certain days, the markets also have sections devoted to clothes and antiques. The best markets are probably those in **Nice** (Cours Saleya in the Old Town), **Cannes** (near Le Suquet and the yacht-harbour), **Antibes** (in the Old Town) — but smaller towns such as **Cagnes-sur-Mer** have lively street-markets too. Go early in the morning so as not to be disappointed — most markets close at mid-day, and the vendors often start packing up at around eleven-thirty.

Bigger street-markets are held over the border in **Vintimille** and **San Remo** (Fridays and Saturdays respectively) — go by car (or train in high-season, if you want to avoid queues at the frontier and parking problems once you get there) — but don't forget your passport or I.D. papers — and, hold on to your purse!

CAFES & RESTAURANTS

Nothing is more pleasant than to sit and watch the world go by from the sunny terrace of a Riviera café. Don't feel obliged to order more than one drink. To be sure of getting what you want, remember that a small beer is called a *demi*, a black coffee is an *express,* but a white coffee is a *café crème.* Prices are generally higher on the terrace than inside the café and may, in some establishments, double in the evening.

From pizza to *nouvelle cuisine* and with over 3000 restaurants, the Riviera is the mecca for diversity in eating. Most retaurants offer a *plat du jour* — a "dish of the day", or a *menu touristique*, which often represents the best choice in terms of being served quickly and in terms of quality. Prices shown in the restaurant may be *service non compris* (service not included, usually added to your bill at 15%) or *service compris/net* (including service charge). In addition, you may want to leave a tip for the waiter (10-15%). At lunch time, good restaurants fill up quickly shortly after noon; in the evening, French people eat from 8 o'clock on.

TOURISM

The coast and the immediate inland region offer an incredible diversity of tourist facilities. Simply be aware that everywhere is crowded in holiday seasons, and be prepared for traffic jams in the vicinity of major tourist sites. For full information, refer to the specific sections of this guide.

If you want to plan trips, go to any accredited travel agent. You will find a branch of **HAVAS** travel agents in **Nice** at 13 Place Masséna (93.62.09.09), **Cannes** (5, rue du Maréchal Foch, Tel: 93.99.33.33) and **Monaco** at 4, rue Iris (93.25.73.73) as well as in many other smaller towns in the area.

ACTIVITIES & CULTURE

To find out about activities and cultural events in each particular town, go to the *Maison de Tourisme* or the *Syndicat d'Initiative* (tourist office). They will give you up-to-date lists and brochures in English or French.

The Riviera has always been an important cultural centre, with a variety of writers, sculptors, artists and film-makers living and working here. In addition, there are a lot of private and public art galleries and exhibitions where you can go to buy or just look. Remember that public art galleries and museums close on Tuesdays. Lists of galleries can be obtained from the *Maison de Tourisme/Syndicat d'initiative.*

The holiday seasons are full of festivals, from local village *fêtes* to the Cannes Film Festival and the Nice Jazz Festival. Programmes indicating what's happening on the *Côte d'Azur* can be found in the **Nice-Matin** (local daily newspaper) or the **Semaine des**

Spectacles, a weekly magazine; both are in French, but you should be able to figure out what's what.

Most foreign films are dubbed in French — even if the title is left in English. Normally, you'll see **V.O.** or **V.O.S.T.F** (*version originale,* sub-titled in French) after the name of the film to indicate that it is in the original language.

Sports include everything from windsurfing to skiing. Refer to the specific section in this guide.

MAGAZINES/NEWSPAPERS/ BOOKS

You can find most regular English or American magazines in many central newspaper shops. Don't be surprised if you have to pay double the normal price for them (always check the "overseas tarif" that is usually indicated somewhere on the cover).

English language books are similarly increased in price by 50-100%, depending on where you buy them. The best bets are English language bookshops; the most expensive are corner newspaper shops or vendors near the beaches.

CANNES ENGLISH BOOKSHOP
10, rue Jean de Riouffe
CANNES
Tel: 93.99.40.08

RIVIERA BOOKSHOP
10, rue Chauvain
NICE
Tel: 93.85.84.61

BRITISH LIBRARY
30, boulevard Moulins
MONACO
Tel: 93.30.77.34

HAIRDRESSERS

Explaining how you want your hair done is never an easy task – especially in French. You'll find a wide choice, including all the big names in French hair stylists **(Dessange, Jean-Louis David**, etc.). Although there is a salon in just about every small town and village, many beauty parlors on the Riviera are open seasonally and almost all of them are closed on Mondays. These are some salons open all year long where you can be assured of a quality cut.

DESSANGE
21, rue Commandant André
CANNES
Tel: 93.67.43.44
37, rue Dubouchage
NICE
Tel: 92.85.81.38

JEAN LOUIS DAVID
21, rue des Etats-Unis
CANNES
Tel: 93.38.58.58
Nice Etoile
Avenue Médecin
NICE
Tel: 93.80.24.20

MAROTTE
21, rue Liberté
NICE
Tel: 93.87.60.90

PHARMACIES/CHEMISTS

Recognisable by the green cross; most pharmacies are open from 9 am to noon, and 2 to 7 pm, Monday through Saturday. Be warned that, unlike most Riviera businesses, pharmacies tend to close right on time. On weekends, when most pharmacies are closed, you need to find the *Pharmacies de garde* (emergency pharmacies open on that particular day). You will find them listed in the **Nice-Matin**, under each city, or in the window of any pharmacy. If you can't find one open at night, call the local police-station (*commissariat*) to ask what to do.

Some drugs which you can get across the counter in other countries may require a doctor's prescription (*ordonnance*) in

France. On the other hand, pharmacies in France employ highly-qualified personnel, who are even authorised to prescribe certain drugs. For minor ailments, many people consult their pharmacist rather than going to a doctor.

EMERGENCIES

Police: dial 17
Fire Brigade: dial 18

S.O.S. Doctor (24-hour service)
Antibes: 93.61.09.09
Cannes: 93.38.10.11 or 93.38.39.38
Nice: 93.83.01.01
Monaco (Ambulance Service): 93.30.04.85

SUNNY BANK HOSPITAL
English Hospital
133, avenue Petit Juas
CANNES
93.68.26.96

CONSULATES

CANADA
24, avenue du Prado
13006 Marseille
Tel: 91.37.19.37

GREAT BRITAIN
11, rue Paradis
06000 Nice
Tel: 93.82.32.04

U.S.A.
31, rue Maréchal Joffre
06000 Nice
Tel: 93.88.89.55

LOST AND FOUND

If you lose your passport/chequebook/credit cards, go to the nearest police station immediately and report it.

Passport: inform the consulate immediately and they will advise you on what action to take.

Credit Cards: inform the credit card company immediately.

It's a good idea to make photocopies of all important documents and leave the originals in the hotel safe. This will greatly simplify the procedure if the worst comes to the worst.

Remember that any holiday place is prime territory for thieves, and the Riviera is no exception: don't leave anything in your car;

be extremely careful with purses, wallets and cameras especially when walking in crowded areas at any time of day.

At the police station, don't get excited: the procedure takes time, there are always a number of people in the same situation as yourself, and as the weather is hot, tempers have a tendency to run short. Remember that the policeman is depending on his school English to understand you, so speak slowly and repeat if necessary.

TELEPHONE

Phone calls within a town cost 1F. However, you'll find that an increasing number of phones only accept a special card of 40 francs worth of phone calls. These are on sale in tobacconists' shops (*tabacs*) and post offices. Insert the card and an electronic system automatically deducts the cost of the call from the balance memorised in the card. Instructions are posted in the phone booth. You can make international calls from any phone booth, but for longer calls and a bit of peace and quiet, it's better to go to the post office: there, you have to go to the specific desk which deals with international phone calls and request a booth. Pay at the desk after making the call. To call abroad dial 19 first, wait for the dial tone and then dial the appropriate country code (Australia=61, Canada=1, New Zealand=64, UK=44, USA=1) followed by the number you wish to reach. For international information dial 19.33 plus the country code.

POST OFFICES

The queues tend to be long and the post office too small and too hot: it's advisable to go there only when essential. Buy stamps in bulk rather than one at a time. You can also buy stamps in *tabacs* — special cafés or newspaper shops which sell cigarettes and display a special red pole outside. Average airmail rates from France for postcards are 1.80 F to the UK and Canada and 2.50 F to the USA, Australia and New Zealand. Letters up to 20 grams can be sent airmail for 2.50 F to the UK, 2.20 F to Canada, and 3.20 F to the USA, Australia and New Zealand. You can send telegrams via your hotel phone rather than going to the post office. To send a telegram dial 36.55 and dictate your message. Telexes can be sent from the central post office in most major towns.

RELIGIOUS SERVICES

ANGLICAN

CANNES
Anglican Church
Rue Général Ferrié
Tel: 93.94.54.61

MONACO
Anglican Church
22, avenue Grande Bretagne
Tel: 93.30.71.06

NICE
The English Church
11, rue Buffa
Tel: 93.87.19.83

CATHOLIC

CANNES
Notre Dame Bon Voyage
Square Mèrimée
Tel: 93.39.16.22

MONACO
The Cathedral
4, rue Colonel Bellando de Castro
Tel: 93.30.88.13

NICE
Notre Dame
Avenue Médecin
Tel: 93.88.73.63

SYNAGOGUES

CANNES
20, boulevard Alsace
Tel: 93.38.16.54

MONACO
15, avenue de la Costa
Tel: 93.30.16.46

NICE
24, rue de France
Tel: 93.82.26.15

T.V./RADIO

Check the T.V. schedules found in local newspapers or in magazines like **Télérama** for films that are in English on one of the 3 national channels that can be picked up in the region (the name of the film is followed by VO or VOSTF in the program).

You'll hear a lot of English songs on the radio, and **Radio Riviera** (broadcasting from Italy at **104.1 FM**) has only English music, with news, weather and stock-exchange information in English every hour.

HOTELS

In holiday seasons, it's not recommended to come without a reservation when almost every hotel on the coast has a *complet* (no vacancies) sign on the door. At other times of the year, you have a wide choice of accommodation. The rating system is by stars, from * to **** *de luxe.* Note that stars followed by NN indicates *Nouvelles Normes,* meaning that the hotel meets modern standards of comfort for each category. If you don't have a reservation, call the Tourist Office in the town concerned.

REGIONAL TOURIST BOARD

NICE: 93.44.50.59

TOURIST OFFICES

CANNES: 93.99.19.77
MONACO: 93.25.73.73
NICE: 93.87.07.07
SAINT-TROPEZ: 94.97.46.66

2
MONACO: THE GLAMOUR AND THE GOLD

30 | Monaco Today
31 | The Making of Monaco
32 | Where To Stay
38 | Interesting Things To Do in Monaco
42 | The Beaches and the Sea
43 | Superlative Shopping
49 | Excursions: Roquebrune-Cap-Martin
Menton
Villefranche-sur-Mer
Saint Jean-Cap Ferrat
Beaulieu
53 | The Grand Excursion: The Corniche Roads

For many visitors, Monaco is synonymous with Monte Carlo, high life and gambling. Monaco is seen as a haven for the very rich, a city of millionaires and princes, ruled over by an always glittering royal family. From behind the lenses of the world's photographers, the world sees a widower Prince and his young and fashionable children, ruling from a cloud-pink castle on the rocks above the sea. Meanwhile, in the town below, from nightspot to nightspot, and yacht to yacht, the beautiful and the powerful mix and meet, to make love, fun and money.

All of this is true, yet not quite true. Monaco is indeed a very unusual city, in a fairy-land décor. The city cascades down the side of the mountain into the sea, all in white and pink pastels, with a stage-set architecture half-way between Sleeping Beauty and Dallas. It is sometimes hard to remember that the place wasn't just built for visitors and for the cameras of the press, as an effective and descreet backdrop for the lives and loves of millionaires and celebrities.

Behind the glittering surface, however, there is a real city to discover. Monaco is a mixture of a complex and surprising history, an imaginative political compromise, and a growing centre for business and leisure. The three are inter-related, and the visitor who understands a little of each aspect will be more aware of how Monaco functions. The real Monaco is more interesting than any magazine article could ever be. The secrets remain secret, because Monaco is, above all, a discreet and private place, but the visitor can see the influences and share in the lifestyle that makes Monaco what it is: rich, expensive, beautiful and smooth.

Monaco Today

Monaco covers slightly less than two square kilometres. Every inch is built on, but the city continues to expand — in two directions, upwards in ever-higher skyscrapers, and outwards into the sea.

The population is just over 27,000. Only 17 per cent are citizens of Monaco, or *Monégasques*. This is not for lack of candidates since *Monégasques* pay no taxes and enjoy assorted other advantages. However, it is not so easy to become one, and those who leave the Principality soon lose their benefits. As a result, the proportion of foreigners continues to rise. The French make up over half the foreign residents and many of those who work here are Italian.

The Making of Monaco

For most of its history, Monaco was an aggressive little state on a wild and inaccessible stretch of coastline. It was seized in 1297 by a certain François Grimaldi from Genoa, and since then, for seven centuries, with occasional ups and downs, there have been Grimaldis on the rock of Monaco, reigning over a tiny community of pirates, peasants, fishermen and smugglers.

Until relatively recently, Monaco was pitifully poor. In 1861, Charles III of Monaco sold Menton and Roquebrune, which had been part of the Principality, to France, to save his independence.

The legend of Monaco, or rather of Monte Carlo, began in earnest in the middle of the last century with the creation of the **Société des Bains de Mer** (**S.B.M.**). Hotels and a casino (with an opera house attached) were built to attract the rich Russian and Central European clientele which was to make Monte Carlo famous. By the turn of the century Monte Carlo boasted some of the finest hotels in Europe.

The **S.B.M.** owns three of the four luxury hotels in Monte Carlo (plus another in Roquebrune-Cap-Martin), the Casino, the Sporting Club and 18 restaurants. It also controls all of the gambling in the Principality.

Getting There

Monaco is easily reached. It is very near the main highway from Nice to the Italian frontier, and from Nice Airport there are public and hotel buses and taxis which cover the 22 kilometres to Monte Carlo in about half an hour. There is also a helicopter service from Nice Airport to Monaco Heliport which takes seven to eight minutes but costs 25O F per person but a mere 19O F if you take out a season ticket. This compares very favorably with the price of a taxi from the airport (which can take over an hour).

Monaco is on the main railway line from Nice into Italy, so there are frequent trains from all the towns on the Riviera. The station is close to the centre of town.

WHERE TO STAY

There is no shortage of hotel-rooms in Monaco and over 80 percent of them are in the luxury and four-star categories. In addition, the *Belle Epoque*, **Metropole de Monaco**, is scheduled to open in the spring of 1987. Prices quoted below do not take into account special tariffs during the off-season or those for groups and conventions. Monaco has a very competitive program when it comes to attracting businessmen, conferences and incentive trips to the Principality and information is available from the **Direction du Tourisme et des Congrès** (2a, boulevard des Moulins, Monte Carlo, Tel: 93.30.87.01).

FOR DEEPER POCKETS

HOTEL HERMITAGE

Square Beaumarchais
Tel: 93.5O.67.31

Built during the *Belle Epoque* , it forms part of the **S.B.M.** empire, and it is virtually impossible to get a room without booking a year in advance. The price of a room for two people with bath, but without breakfast, ranges from 75O F to 16OO F depending on the room and the time of year. All hotels charge more than their normal maximum during the Grand Prix.

HOTEL DE PARIS

Place du Casino
Tel: 93.5O.8O.8O

The oldest, but by far the grandest hotel in the **S.B.M.** group although it seems to be permanently under renovation. Glamourously situated, next-door to the Casino, it still attracts a glittering clientele from all over the world. Double rooms from 860 F to 1850 F. As in all of the *de luxe* hotels, breakfast is extra (86.25 F per person).

HOTEL MIRABEAU

1/3, avenue Princesse Grace
Tel: 93.25.45.45

Situated near the Larvotto Beach, this is Monaco's newest hotel and the furnishings are modern-American. It has an excellent restaurant with a dessert menu that will leave visions of sugar plum fairies dancing in your head long after you've left the Principality. Prices for a double-room range from 690 F to 1322 F.

LOEWS MONTE CARLO

12, avenue des Spélugues
Tel: 93.50.65.00

The most American of Monaco's hotels. Everything is up on the roof: an excellent restaurant, the casino and you can even swim under the stars in January in the heated pool. 636 rooms, the price of which range from 930 F to 1750 F according to season. Breakfast extra.

METROPOLE DE MONACO

17, Galerie Charles III
Tel: 93.50.15.10

Rebuilt on the site of the old Metropole and meticulously re-created to evoke all the charm and luxury of the *Belle Epoque.* Although not opening until the spring of 1987, this 19th-century castle promises to be one of the Principality's most elegant hotels. 150 *de luxe* rooms and suites, boutiques, offices, apartments, a heated, indoor-outdoor swimming pool. Probably the safest place on the *Côte* , it has even been built with a fall-out shelter and earthquake stabilizers! Located in the center of the city, on the *Carré d'Or*, overlooking the gardens of the Casino. Sorry, but we don't have the prices yet.

MONTE CARLO BEACH

Route du Beach
ROQUEBRUNE
Tel: 93.78.21.40

Also owned by the **S.B.M.** but situated just across the border in Roquebrune. Often referred to as the *Old* Beach to differentiate it from the Beach Plaza. Prices are only a little lower than those in Monaco but there are only fifty rooms. However, there is an Olympic swimming pool with heated sea-water. Often frequented by the royal princesses or used as a backdrop for Helmut Newton's exotic/erotic photos. An extremely fashionable private beach.

BEACH PLAZA

22, avenue Princesse Grace
Tel: 93.38.98.80

This is the only 4-star hotel in Monte Carlo owned by Trust House-Forte. As its name suggests, it is right on the beach which is private and considered to be the best in the

Principality. Rooms with bath cost from 1000 F in the low season up to 1700 F in the middle of July, inclusive of service and all taxes. Breakfast 55 F.

MORE MODEST SELECTIONS (3*)

HOTEL ALEXANDRA

35, boulevard Princesse Charlotte
Tel: 93.50.63.13

Convenient to the centre of the town. A total of 55 rooms. Daily rates for a double room with shower between 285 F and 325 F. No restaurant.

LE BALMORAL

12, avenue de la Costa
Tel: 93.50.62.37

Probably the best in this category, with 68 rooms of which some have a lovely view over the old harbor. Air-conditioned restaurant. Double-room with bath 360-500 F per night.

HOTEL DU LOUVRE

16, boulevard des Moulins
Tel: 93.50.65.25

34 air-conditioned rooms, all with bath, in the main shopping street of Monaco. Double room: 408-495 F.

HOTEL MIRAMAR

1, avenue Président J. F. Kennedy
Tel: 93.30.86.48

A small, recently renovated hotel, possibly the most attractively situated in this category, right on the old harbor. 14 air-conditioned double-rooms, all with bath, from 450 F to 510 F.

FOR SMALLER WALLETS (2* & 1*)

Double-rooms in the 2-star category in Monaco cost between 230 and 300 F per night, and in the 1-star category (with shower) from 132 to 230 F. If you go broke playing roulette, head for the last hotel on our list.

HOTEL LE SIECLE

10, avenue Prince Pierre
Tel: 93.30.25.56

2-stars, 39 rooms not far from the railway station and the old market on the Place d'Armes.

HOTEL DE LA POSTE

5, rue des Oliviers
Tel: 93.30.70.56

22 rooms, none with private bathroom facilities, but charging a mere 76-84 F per night for a double-room.

HOTELS WITHIN STRIKING DISTANCE OF MONACO

LE VISTAERO
Route de la Grande Corniche
ROQUEBRUNE-CAP-MARTIN
Tel: 93.35.01.50

De luxe 4-star hotel which seems to be rather dangerously perched on a cliff overlooking the bay with an incredible view from Monaco to Bordighera in Italy.

HOTEL VICTORIA ET DE LA PLAGE
7, promenade du Cap
CAP MARTIN
Tel: 93.35.65.90

A comfortable 3-star hotel on Cap Martin.

HOTEL ALEXANDRA
Avenue Sir Winston Churchill
CAP MARTIN
Tel: 93.35.65.45

Another 3-star hotel in an avenue named after an illustrious fan of Roquebrune-Cap-Martin. King Umberto of Italy, Coco Chanel and Greta Garbo, among others, were all attracted by its temperate climate, healthy air and luxuriant vegetation. Their villas are dotted about the Cape which is probably best visited on foot.

MENTON

There are no *de luxe* or four-star establishments in here, but of the 4O hotels there are 7 with three stars which are worth considering.

Le Napoléon
Tel: 93.35.89.50
Considered the best hotel in Menton.

Le Chambord
Tel: 93.35.94.19

Hôtel Du Parc
Tel: 93.57.66.66

L'Europ Hotel
Tel: 93.35.59.92

Le Mediterranée
Tel: 93.28. 25.25

Le Viking
Tel: 93.57. 95.85

Le Prince de Galles
Tel: 93.28.21.21

— "Maman! I'm bored.

sempé.

INTERESTING THINGS TO DO IN MONACO

Most of the historical sights to be seen are up on the Rock, as the rest of Monaco is very much a twentieth-century phenomenon. If you intend to do Monaco in a day, remember to wear comfortable shoes, as the walking is of the up-and-down variety.

EXPLORING THE ROCK

THE PRINCE'S PALACE

Napoleonic Museum
Palace Archives
Place du Palais
MONACO-VILLE
Palace: Adults 20 F, kids 10 F
Museum/Archives: 10 F & 5 F

Occupying a splendid site at the top of the Rock, and partially open to the public. Some interesting items to be seen in the Museum and Archives. At the main entrance, the **Changing of the Guard** takes place daily at 11:55 am sharp.

THE OCEANOGRAPHIC MUSEUM AND AQUARIUM

Avenue Saint Martin
Adults 40 F, kids & students 20 F

One of the most interesting sights in the Principality. Even those who normally find fish boring are immensely impressed by this museum. Founded in 1910 by Prince Albert I, the Scientist-Prince, it is currently under the direction of **Jacques-Yves Cousteau** whose films are shown in the conference hall. It is well worth the detour, as *Michelin* puts it.

THE OLD TOWN OF MONACO

Also well worth a visit. It is Italianate in character but kept immaculate and well painted. There also some excellent small restaurants. A pleasant public garden, **Le Jardin Saint Martin,** facing the sea.

MONACO CATHEDRAL

4, rue Colonel Bellando de Castro

Built shortly after Monaco separated fron the diocese of Nice in 1868, and a monument to the taste of 1875. However, there is a very beautiful painting by the *Niçois* artist, Louis Bréa, dating from about 1500.

FORT ANTOINE THEATRE

Avenue de la Quarantaine

An early 18th century fortress on

the north-east tip of the Rock which serves today as an open-air theatre. Intimate concerts held on summer evenings for those lucky enough to get one of the 350 available tickets.

IN AND AROUND THE CASINO

THE CASINO AND THE OPERA HOUSE (Salle Garnier)

A magical sight at night when the lights are turned on. Really a wonderful building. Even if you don't intend to gamble, and you're over 21, pay a (free) visit to the Casino which was built in 1878 by Charles Garnier, architect of *l'Opera de Paris*. There is also a costume museum.

In addition to opera, Monaco offers concerts, ballet performances and recitals all year round, often with world-renowned soloists, though it has to be said that at times the resident **Monte Carlo Philharmonic Orchestra** leaves something to be desired. The **Monte Carlo Ballet Company** is world-famous and there are often good plays at the **Théâtre Princesse Grace**, though mostly in French.

RAINIER III CONGRESS CENTRE

A fine example of Monaco's very successful efforts to provide business-tourism with the most attractive and up-to-date convention facilities. Films are sometimes shown here and in some of the museums. The cinema, **Le Sporting d'Hiver** (in the building that also houses Sotheby's Auction Rooms opposite the Casino Gardens) sometimes shows undubbed foreign films. In summer, there is a great open-air cinema at the **Monte Carlo Sporting Club**, situated at the far end of the avenue Princesse Grace.

FOR NATURE LOVERS

THE ZOOLOGICAL GARDENS

At the foot of the Rock
Adults 10 F, kids 5 F

Possibly more of interest from a flora than a fauna point of view. Situated in one of the many beneficial micro-climates that exist on the Riviera, there are some very unusual plants as well as a few animals.

THE EXOTIC GARDENS AND MUSEUM OF PREHISTORIC ANTHROPOLOGY

Adults 24 F, students 15.50 F, kids 12 F

Situated at the northern entrance to the Principality, via the *Moyenne Corniche*. Devoted almost entirely to succulents and cacti, the Garden has been hit by two hard winters in succession and now has taken to protecting certain plants with screens

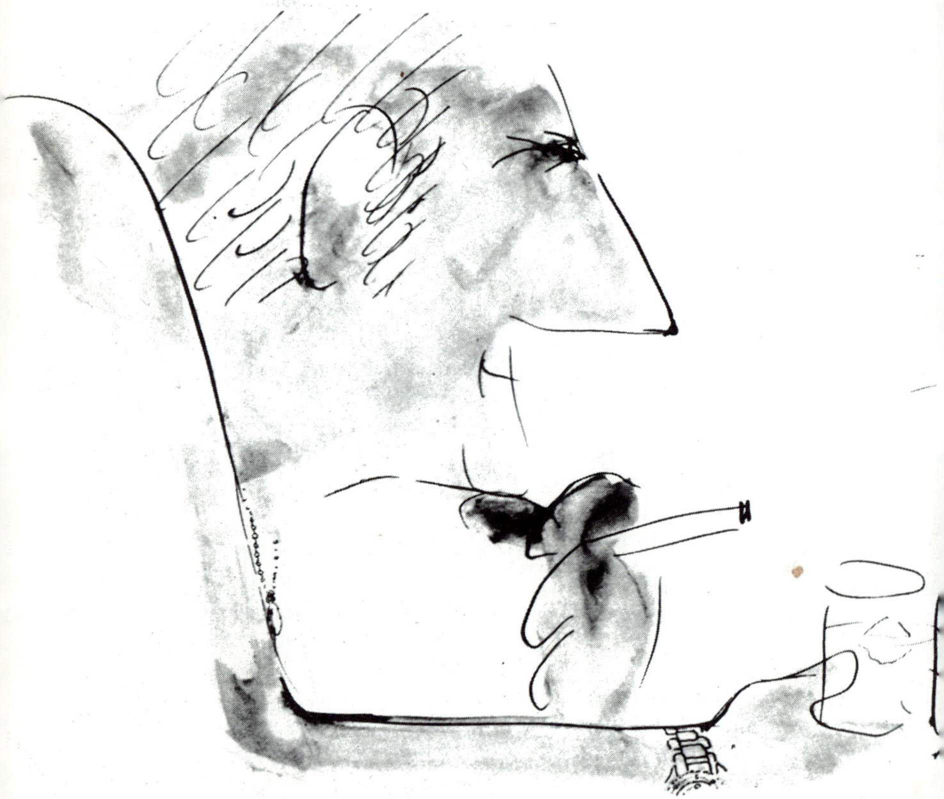

and fibreglass wrapping during the winter months. Resist the temptation to steal cuttings; either you will be pricked to bits or reprimanded by guards watching the more *amenable* plants. Below the gardens and open to the public are pre-historic caves with well-lit stalagmites, stalagtites.

THE BEACHES AND THE SEA

There are virtually no free beaches in the Principality. There are four paying beaches on the **Plage du Larvotto**, which is about 450 metres long and consists of land reclaimed from the sea. These beaches charge a reasonable 35 F per day including a sun-mattress. You will find addresses and telephone numbers under **Where to Stay in Monaco**.

THE BEACH PLAZA

Charges 55 F per day but you must have someone to invite you who is staying at the hotel.

MONTE CARLO BEACH

Where to see the royal princesses, assorted stars from the worlds of tennis, racing, films... The most expensive of the paying beaches. A season ticket (from 1 June-6 Sept) can cost upwards of 20,000 F depending on the luxury demanded. A day-ticket is around 100 F including a sun-mattress. If you stay in an **S.B.M.** hotel, this beach is included in the price of the room. The restaurant and bars on this beach are **S.B.M.**-owned and priced accordingly.

MONTE CARLO SEA CLUB

20, avenue Princesse Grace

A bathing-complex ideal for kids, but unfortunately only open to season-ticket holders.

THE CALIFORNIA TERRACE

Avenue de Monte Carlo

A very beautiful heated indoor pool, with an elegant terrace overlooking the harbour, and the latest in modern health-spa facilities. Wonderful health food restaurant.

LE STADE NAUTIQUE RAINIER III

A fine open-air swimming-pool, situated behind the old yacht-harbor. Very reasonable fees.

CAP D'AIL

A few minutes' drive from Monaco on the way back to Nice. This rocky cove is extremely picturesque and has several paying beaches with mattresses and parasols to rent at slightly cheaper prices than in Monaco. A pebble beach at the foot of a good number of steps. The climb back up at the end of the day can be exhausting.

CAP MARTIN AND MENTON

Pleasant beaches and coves to be found all around and long stretches of beach and promenades.

SUPERLATIVE SHOPPING

Monte Carlo is a shopper's paradise. Virtually all the big names are there but there are also many private shops and jewellers who provide excellent design and quality at relatively reasonable prices. It is not the place to seek bargains although at sale time, January and July, even these are available to the lucky passer-by.

All the shops are open by 10 am and most close at the latest at 12:30 for lunch. All shops are open again by 3 pm and remain so until at least 7 and sometimes until 7:30. Most shops are open all day Saturday unless there is mention to the contrary. Most of the jewellers open at 10:00 am and most of the boutiques at 9:30 am.

The list below is a sampling. We could have listed twice as many and still not covered the variety of luxury goods available in the Monaco shopping areas. Charge cards have been abbreviated as follows: Amex= American Express; D=Diners Club; V=Visa, Carte Bleue, etc.; MC=Mastercard, Access, Eurocard; JCB=JCB a Japanese credit card.

HIGH-CLASS JEWELLERS IN THE CASINO AREA

Place du Casino

CARTIER
Tel: 93.30.86.58
Cards: Amex/D/V/MC

Jewellery and leather goods. Mostly devoted to their **Must** boutique but special jewellery orders accepted.

REPOSSI
Tel: 93.50.80.80
Cards: Amex

Boutique in the **Hôtel de Paris**. Also has a shop for more serious things in the **Hôtel Hermitage**. Tel: 93.50.89.59.

ALBUQUERQUE
Tel: 93.50.62.90
Cards: Amex/D/V/MC

Jewellers and silversmiths. One of the oldest establishments in Monte Carlo but there is nothing old fashioned about their merchandise.

VAN CLEEF AND ARPELS
TEL: 93.50.54.08.
Cards: Amex/D

Well-known for modern designs and invisible settings. Also has a boutique for less expensive jewellery.

Avenue des Beaux Arts

A short street less than 150 meters long but absolutely packed with the BIG names in fashion and design.

BULGARI
Tel: 93.50.88.40
Cards: Amex/D/V

Probably the most famous Italian jewellers in the world, whose designs are copied by so many others.

YVES ST. LAURENT RIVE GAUCHE
Tel: 93.30.18.19
Cards: Amex/D/V

Stock their latest ready-to-wear collection with additions for the Mediterranean climate.

CHRISTIAN DIOR
Tel: 93.50.92.04
Cards: Amex/D/V

All the latest ready-to-wear plus very beautiful furs next door.

GIVENCHY
Tel: 93.25.34.04.
Cards: Amex/D/V

A relative new-comer to Monaco. Probably the best quality ready-to-wear available but at almost *haute couture* prices.

LOUIS VUITTON
Tel: 93.25.13.44
Cards: Amex/D/V/MC

Luggage and handbags. Apart from the ubiquitous LV logo, Vuitton now makes luggage in exciting plain colours such as emerald, royal blue, yellow and scarlet.

BUCCELATI
Tel: 93.50.90.10
Cards: Amex

Jewellers and silversmiths. A top Italian house with shops all over Europe and America. Beautiful designed silverware.

RIBOLZI
Tel: 93.30.06.25
No cards

Antiques. Owned by an architect turned antique-dealer. Has another shop in Lugano, Switzerland. Mainly Italian and French items.

Avenue de Monte Carlo

A very select row of boutiques, just around the corner from the Casino and facing the sea.

VALENTINO
Tel: 93.25.12.63
Cards: Amex/D/V

Ready-to-wear collection. Also does handbags and leather goods and there is a man's shop just round the corner at Square Beaumarchais.

HERMES
Tel: 93.5O.64.89
Cards: Amex/D/V/MC

Leather goods and ready-to-wear. Their scarves are world famous and they have recently re-issued some of those designed in 1937. Also stock **Lobb of London** shoes for men.

JEAN LOUIS SCHERRER
Tel: 93.50.85.83
Cards: Amex/D/V

Ready-to-wear collection. Classic top quality Paris fashions. Also take orders for their *Haute Couture.*

CARLO TIVOLI
Tel: 93.25.05.02
No cards

All Italian beautifully designed jewellery from their workshops in Turin and Milan.

M. GERARD
Tel: 93.30.05.06
No cards

Jeweller. Well-known, exclusive and very expensive designer.

Boulevard des Moulins

The main shopping street in Monte Carlo, with a wide variety of boutiques starting at the Casino end (and to mention but a few).

LOUIS SCIOLLA
Tel: 93.50.50.61
Cards: Amex/V/D/MC

MONACO

Tailors and menswear. This is a *Monégasque* firm but with branches in Cannes and Nice. Many Italian imports.

PARFUMERIE HELDER

Tel: 93.30.65.10
Cards: Amex/D/V/MC

Perfumes and beauty products, all makes including **Guerlain.**

JANE

Tel: 93.50.15.65
Cards: D/V

Ready-to-wear fashions. Stocks **Chloé** and **Nina Ricci** boutique models.

SAPJO

Tel: 93.50.54.34
Cards: Amex/D/V/MC/JCB
Undoubtedly the best antique shop in Monte Carlo. Specializes in antique silver and rare porcelain.

CHARLES JOURDAN

Tel: 93.50.86.51
Cards: Amex/D/V/MC
High fashion shoes, boots and beautiful scarves.

LORIS AZZARO

Tel: 93.30.00.62
Cards: Amex/D/V

Ready-to-wear fashion. Beautiful evening knits and evening shoes not available elsewhere.

DANA COTE D'AZUR

Tel: 93.30.82.56
Cards: Amex/D/V/MC

Casual but expensive *prêt à porter* . Also do *Haute Couture* to order.

CHARLOTTE

Tel: 93.50.53.89
Cards: Amex/V

Fashion. Part of a French chain which buys in large quantities and therefore prices are very reasonable for Monte Carlo. Stocks the German house of **Fink, Pierre Cardin, Pierre Balmain, Sym** and **Caroll** knits.

TRUSSARDI

Tel: 93.25.41.70
Cards: Amex/D/V/MC/JCB

Beautifully made Italian handbags and travel goods.

SALGANIK

Tel: 93.50.51.19
Closed Saturdays in summer.
Cards: Amex/D

Furs, *Haute Couture* and *Prêt à porter*. Apart from making their own furs they also import Grosvenor of Canada minks and sables.

AU GRAND ECHANSON

Tel: 93.50.61.19
No cards

A very comprehensive selection of wines from both France and Italy including several Burgundies which do not normally figure on southern wine lists.

Les Allées Lumières

Elegant shopping precinct in the Park Palace building, 27, avenue de la Costa (a continuation west of the boulevard des Moulins, at the top of the Casino Gardens). Mostly (expensive) fashion boutiques for women.

ZOE
Tel: 93.25.04.35
Cards: Amex/D/V/MC
Stocks **Hanae Mori** and **Déjac**.

JEAN JACQUES
Tel: 93.50.87.85
Cards: Amex/D

Menswear. Imported **Burberrys, Daks, Chester Barrie** as well as Scottish knitwear.

GIANFRANCO FERRE
Tel: 93.25.61.05
Cards: Amex/D/V/MC

The latest star of Italian fashion now has a shop in Monte Carlo.

MAROTTE
Tel: 93.25.10.37

Prêt à porter and accessories. Stocks all the big Italian names, **Gucci, Valentino, Fendi** plus **Borsalino** for men.

MORABITO
Tel: 93.25.11.80
Cards: Amex/D/V/MC

Prêt à porter. Also famous for his studded luggage and jewellery.

GIANNI VERSACE
Tel: 93.25.13.40
Cards: Amex/D/V

Another darling of Italian fashion with very wearable designs.

KANSAI
Tel: 93.25.30.51
Cards: Amex/D/V/MC/JCB

Very fashionable and expensive designer for fans of the *avant-garde*.

MAZZOCCA
Tel: 93.30.51.61
Cards: Amex/D/V

Ready-to-wear for men and women. A great deal of Italian imports including **Missoni, Enzo Russo** and **Ginocchietti**. Some of the best knits in Monte Carlo. Also stocks furs by **Viscardi** and **Melegari Costa.**

LOUIS FERAUD
Tel: 93.25.32.40
Cards: Amex/D/V

Prêt à porter. Excellent design at comparatively reasonable prices.

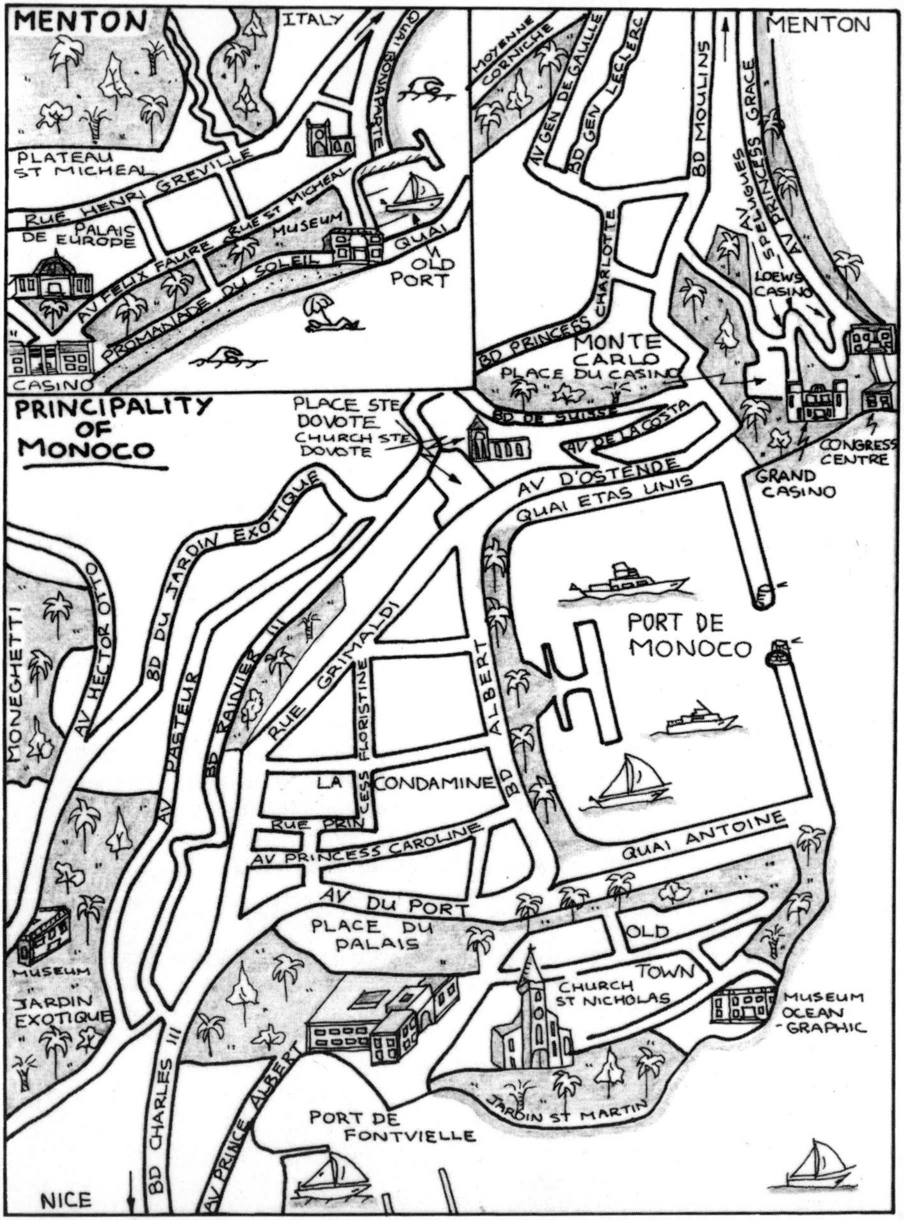

MENTON
ITALY
QUAI BONAPARTE
PLATEAU ST MICHEAL
RUE HENRI GREVILLE
RUE ST MICHEAL
PALAIS DE EUROPE
MUSEUM
AV FELIX FAURE
PROMANADE DU SOLEIL
QUAI
OLD PORT
CASINO
MOYENNE CORNICHE
AV GEN DE GAULLE
BD GEN LECLERC
BD MOULINS
MENTON
AV PRINCESS GRACE
AV SPELUGUES
BD CHARLOTTE
BD PRINCESS CHARLOTTE
LOEWS CASINO
MONTE CARLO
PLACE DU CASINO
PRINCIPALITY OF MONOCO
PLACE STE DOVOTE
CHURCH STE DOVOTE
BD DE SUISSE
AV DE LA COSTA
CONGRESS CENTRE
GRAND CASINO
AV D'OSTENDE
QUAI ETAS UNIS
BD DU JARDIN EXOTIQUE
AV HECTOR OTTO
MONEGHETTI
PORT DE MONOCO
BD RAINIER III
RUE GRIMALDI
AV PASTEUR
CESS FLORISTINE
BD ALBERT
LA CONDAMINE
RUE PRIN
AV PRINCESS CAROLINE
QUAI ANTOINE
AV DU PORT
PLACE DU PALAIS
OLD TOWN
CHURCH ST NICHOLAS
MUSEUM
JARDIN EXOTIQUE
MUSEUM OCEAN-GRAPHIC
BD CHARLES III
AV PRINCE ALBERT
JARDIN ST MARTIN
PORT DE FONTVIELLE
NICE

EXCURSIONS

Roquebrune-Cap-Martin

The history of **Roquebrune** was much the same as that of the Principality of Monaco until 1860 when it was sold back to France. Once a halting place for the Knights Templar, there are still historic buildings to be visited including a 12th century castle, the **Basilique Saint Martin** and a Templar Chapel. The place can be said to be divided in two parts, that of the old village perched high up in the hills (where there are one or two good restaurants) and that of **Cap Martin**, at sea level, world famous for its luxurious villas, beautiful gardens and the people who have come here to live.

In the summer it is a very lively place but by October 1st, although the climate is still excellent, the resort atmosphere has disappeared and Cap Martin becomes something of a geriatric resort. It cheers up slightly over Christmas and the New Year when the restaurants and hotels temporarily re-open. There is then a lull until Easter, when everthing comes to life once more. There is a daily market in both Roquebrune and in Cap Martin but neither place can be labelled as anything but ordinary as far as shopping is concerned. However, there are a few *brocante* (not quite junk, but not really antique) shops in the old town.

Menton

Menton has a Casino and a very faithful holiday clientele in summer. It has good public and private beaches (virtually all pebbles) and one or two excellent restaurants. **Chez Régine** near the port of Menton is probably the best beach but there is also another good one, **La Solenzara**, towards Cap Martin. However, the mean age of Menton is 77 and the pace on the pavements is distinctly slow. Although it has an excellent, mild climate and a first-class marina built in the sheltered **Baie de Garavan**, there is very little going on in Menton out of season. Nevertheless, it is a good place to stay when exploring the back-country or nearby Italy.

There are daily markets in Menton and a particularly good one near the *Gare Routière*. Both **Prisunic** and **Nouvelles Galeries** have stores in the town. However, it has to be said that for serious shopping a lot of *Mentonnais* go either to Italy or to Nice, where the choice is greater and the prices lower.

SAINTE AGNES, which is the highest village on the *Côte d'Azur*, is worth a visit as are other mountainous retreats such as **LA TURBIE** and **TENDE**.

Villefranche-sur-Mer

In a very civilised setting, **Villefranche**, on the sea between Nice and Monaco, is one of the oldest and most respectable resorts of the Riviera, chosen in the last century as a Mediterranean base for the Imperial Russian Navy. With this choice came Grand Dukes and other nobles, followed by the rest of Europe's high society. The traces of their passage are all around, in some of the most extravagant and romantic villas of the Riviera, floating in a sea of greenery above the very blue waters of the **Bay of Villefranche.**

The old town, once only a fishing-village, is very much unchanged, and the **Port of Villefranche** is one of the nicest possible places to have a leisurely lunch, in one of the waterfront bistrots. The port is dominated by the 16th century **Citadelle**, with no less than two museums (**Volti** and **Goetz-Boumeester Foundation**, with paintings and sculptures). The **Chapelle Saint Pierre** was decorated by Cocteau, who loved Villefranche dearly.

If you want to stay in Villefranche, you can choose between three three-star hotels: the **HOTEL VERSAILLES** on the Avenue Princesse Grace de Monaco (Tel: 93.01.89.56), with a swimming-pool, from 250 to 500 F a day for a double-room; **LE WELCOME** on the Quai Courbet (Tel: 93.55.27.27), from 200 to 460 F a day; and **LES OLIVETTES** on Avenue Léopold II (Tel: 93.01.71.20), around 345 F for a double room with a bath and sea view.

Saint Jean – Cap Ferrat

One side of the **Bay of Villefranche** is formed by the narrow peninsula of **Cap Ferrat**, which hasn't changed much in the last fifty years. As with the Cap d'Antibes and the Cap Martin, the land has remained in the hands of the very rich, who have maintained their beautiful grounds and gardens in the spirit they were originally intended.

Those who are not lucky enough to have land-owning friends on the Cap can still enjoy its greenery and the atmosphere of discreet wealth. You can even walk all the way around the cape on the numerous small roads and footpaths in the shadow of vegetation, a few feet from the waves. Start at the **Plage de Passable** on the western side and meander out to the lighthouse and on to **Saint Jean**.

The **Plage de Passable** is at the end of the Chemin de Passable. Parking is very difficult, but if you manage it, the beach is very nice. You can water-ski, and there is snack-bar with reasonable prices on the beach.

Better still, you can stay at the **GRAND HOTEL DE CAP FERRAT**, at the end of the Cap near the lighthouse (boulevard Général de Gaulle, Tel: 93.01.04.54), which has its own beach (as well as a swimming-pool and tennis-courts). A double-room with half-board (obligatory in season) around 2290 F a day. If this is a bit over your budget, don't try **LA VOILE D'OR** on the Port de Plaisance of Saint Jean (Tel: 93.01.06.62), where the same thing could cost you 3,000 F a day!

Saint Jean itself is a very pleasant little village, with a fishing-fleet, but somewhat overcrowded in summer.

Beaulieu

Across the Cap from Villefranche, **Beaulieu** is perhaps the most *refined* of all the resorts of the Riviera. The **Casino** is certainly one of the most elegant, even from the outside, and the hotels and restaurants operate in a style that has long been forgotten elsewhere.

Beaulieu is well known for its **antique shops**, on the boulevard Maréchal Leclerc. Many of the dealers are interior decorators as well, and this shows in their tasteful window displays and showrooms. There are some good *prêt-à-porter* boutiques on the charming **Port de Plaisance**.

The biggest tourist-attraction is actually a fake, an extraordinary imitation, the **Villa Kerylos**. It is a detailed reconstruction of an ancient Greek villa, decorated with frescos and real Greek antiques. Much better than the real thing!

The two most famous hotels in Beaulieu are the **METROPOLE** (Tel: 93.01.00.08) and **LA RESERVE** (Tel: 93.01.00.01), both overlooking the sea, with excellent restaurants, and both charging accordingly (close to 2000 F half-board for two in the high season). Luckily for some, there is an alternative: **LA RESIDENCE**, on the avenue Albert 1er (Tel: 93.01.06.02), a modern hotel in a residential area, less than 200 yards from the sea and the casino. A double room with bath is 560 F in the high season.

June Freeman

JUNE FREEMAN lives on the Riviera and writes books about travel and life in France.

THE GRAND EXCURSION: THE CORNICHE ROADS

The bare term, the Corniche Road is generally understood to refer to the greatest road of them all, La Grande Corniche... "a road devoted to the seeker after pleasure. People traverse it, not with the object of arriving at a particular destination, but for the delight of the road itself, of the joy it gives to the eye and to the imagination."

Sir Frederick Treves

Sergeant-Surgeon to His Majesty the King
1921

For raw drama of mountains and sea, take the Corniche roads between Nice and Menton. There are three alternative routes, a distance of about 20 miles whichever one you try, running more or less parallel and skirting the sides of mountains that plunge steeply into the sea.

The **Grande Corniche** (sometimes called the *Corniche Supérieure*) is the highest of the three, rising to more than 1,500 feet at one point. It follows the tracks of the Via Julius Augustus, along which the Roman legions marched 2,000 years ago. The Romans were the first tourists who came to take the waters at Cimiez in Nice. The views are described by the guide books as breathtaking. I can't think of a better expression.

The **Moyenne Corniche** is the middle road. It's relatively modern. The views are no less spectacular, and it's the fastest road if you're in a hurry.

The **Basse Corniche** (sometimes called the *Corniche Inférieure*) is the road along the coast and serves the resorts of Villefranche, Cap d'Ail, Beaulieu, Monte-Carlo, Roquebrune-Cap-Martin and Menton.

Which one you take depends on where you live and where you want to go. For example, if you are staying in Nice and have a dinner date in Monte-Carlo, you might take the Moyenne Corniche from Nice in the early evening, climb gradually up the cliff-front

to **Eze-Village** and swing down through the gardens and the orange-trees to **Cap d'Ail** on the coast, a few kilometers from Monaco. This way you miss the commuter (not to mention tourist) traffic along the coast, but don't miss any of the views. Going home after dinner, you might prefer to take the Basse Corniche, stopping off at the elegant **Casino de Beaulieu** or for a drink on the waterfront at **Villefranche**.

There are half a dozen access roads between the three Corniches, so you can zoom up and down from one level to another. Although you can drive the whole length of the Grande Corniche, few people do: generally you use it to reach the village of **La Turbie** or a particular restaurant.

Remember, however, that these roads *are* built on the walls of cliffs, and it is not always possible to get from one town to another directly. For example, the village of **Eze** is in two parts, one on the cliff-top, and the other by the sea, and the only direct access between the upper and lower parts of Eze is on foot (or by mule, a form of transport organized by the **Château Eze** hotel in upper Eze from the station on the coast). It's a picturesque walk among pines and olive-trees and takes about an hour from **Eze-Village** to the sea. There is some jocular talk in the village that another hotelier has plans to build a funicular railway or an elevator. You never know.

The completion of the Moyenne Corniche in 1913 breathed new life into **Monte Carlo** — which at the turn of the century was no larger than Villefranche — and opened up the Corniche region to the outside world.

The next 50 years was the golden age of aristocratic tourism. Winter was the high season in those days, and no self-respecting monarch, minister or industrial tycoon could afford not to put in an appearance at a resort like Monte Carlo or Menton. There are echos of this elitist past in the ornate wedding-cake façades of the hotels and casinos and the Edwardian villas tucked away behind the bougainvillea between the Basse and the Moyenne Corniches.

The Basse Corniche was especially popular with the Russian nobility, who streamed down from Saint Petersburg in private railroad cars. Czar Nicholas was one of the first property speculators. His nephew, Prince Stroganoff, had a villa at **Eze-sur-Mer**.

The statue of Queen Victoria in **Menton** is a reminder of the upper-crust British who were attracted by the mild winters and the gaming tables.

On the Road

One possible route in exploring the Corniche roads is to drive east from Nice on the N98, following the signs to the Basse Corniche. The road hugs the coast all the way to Monte Carlo, taking you past the resorts of Villefranche, Beaulieu, Eze-sur-Mer and Cap d'Ail.

Across the harbor of Villefranche is the wooded peninsula of St. Jean-Cap-Ferrat, which can be reached by turning right on the D25 across a causeway. From Monte Carlo the road climbs gently into densely wooded countryside. There are superb views of Monaco and the sweep of the bay back to Cap d'Ail.

Follow the signs to Cap Martin (D52). The road around the cape is flanked with luxuriant gardens of palms, pines and ancient olive trees. On the right as you swing toward Roquebrune-Cap-Martin you can see Menton with its backdrop of mountains and the Italian Riviera as far as Bordighera. Roquebrune merges into Menton along the beach front.

Leave Menton by avenue Carnot and avenue de la Madone (N7). Take the right fork (D2564), which climbs up past the medieval village of Roquebrune to the Grande Corniche.

ROQUEBRUNE VILLAGE: A finely preserved medieval village with a castle, and dungeons with chains. The church of Sainte Marguerite dates from the 13th century.

Stop to enjoy the view at the Belvedere du Vistaero. Three miles farther on is the village of La Turbie.

LA TURBIE: The famous Roman relic, the Trophy of Augustus, a big block of stone in a high circle of columns, was built in 6 B.C. to commemorate Augustus Caesar's victory over pretty much everyone else in the region. From the ruins you can see Monte Carlo and the coast.

An alternative route from Monte Carlo is via Cap d'Ail. You follow the signs for La Turbie and the Grande Corniche, and the road climbs steeply through hairpin bends. From La Turbie take the left fork to the Moyenne Corniche into the medieval village of Eze perched on the mountain-side.

EZE-VILLAGE: The steeply terraced streets abound with boutiques, bars and bistros. The 14th century Chapelle des Penitents Blancs has a fine 1258 Catalan crucifix. There is an 18th century church with a splendid statue of the Assumption. The Chevre d'Or hotel, in the heart of the old village, has wonderful rooms and one of the best restaurants of the whole Corniche area, as well as a view that can almost distract you from your food. On a clear day, you can see Corsica from the village of Eze.

Leaving Eze, make a right on the D46, which climbs up to the Col d'Eze on the Grande Corniche at its highest point (1.800 feet). There is a stone cross at the side of the road commemorating Pope Pius VII's return from exile in 1814. Three-quarters of a mile farther on is the Belvedere d'Eze. From here you have a great view of the Alps and the Cote d'Azur as far as Saint Tropez.

The last seven miles of the Grande Corniche are spectacular. The hillside is covered with pines and olive trees and there are intermittent views of the Alps as the road winds down toward Nice — an impressive urban panorama, especially at night.

Roger Collis

ROGER COLLIS, writer, broadcaster and resident on the Riviera, writes the business-travel column for the"International Herald Tribune".

Sempé

3
NICE: THE SUNTANNED QUEEN OF THE RIVIERA

63 | Where to Stay in Nice
66 | The Beaches and the Sea
67 | A Walk on the Sunny Side of History
72 | Pleasant Ways to Watch the World Go By
73 | Something to Take Home
77 | Excursions from Nice

NICE

Nobody ever forgets their first view of Nice on the way into the city from the airport: the gentle curve of the **Baie des Anges** (the Bay of Angels), the **Promenade des Anglais**, which seems to go on for ever, vanishing into the haze coming off the blue, blue sea. The rustle of the wind in the palm trees, and luxury hotels glittering with sophistication and refinement, including the ultimate Riviera hotel, the **Negresco**, the luxurious, the famous. Liveried footmen in brimmed hats and white gloves open the doors of Rolls and Porsches, to sweep you into a world of crystal chandeliers. Its main restaurant, the **Chantecler** is rated as one of the best in France, under the supervision of its brilliant young chef, Maximin.

The ancient Greek city of Nikaïa, the Italian town of Nizza, the resort of kings and queens, is now also a modern business-centre preparing for the 21st century. Nice is more than a city; it's a mosaic of lifestyles, nationalities and architecture. Nice is all things to all people, a city where suntanned models in open sports cars drive past the stately mansions of the nineteenth century, where *la crème de la crème* mix with beach-bums and ski-bums off the slopes, the high-tech capital of the South East where science and technology are discussed in the sunshine, under the pine trees and the palms.

The palm-lined avenue, Promenade des Anglais was so baptised in the nineteenth century to honour the English who used used to go for walks along the seashore. In those days, the population considered this to be a very odd occupation. Nowadays, everybody does it, including roller-skaters, joggers, dog-owners, and other fanatics. For the idle visitor, there's even a little wooden train which drives the whole length of the Promenade, stopping at all the points of interest. If you come to Nice by car, and don't want to brave the traffic, you can leave your vehicle at a big car-park a little east of the airport, and take this train to the **Jardin Albert Premier** in the heart of Nice (or take a bus, if you want to get there faster).

The Jardin Albert 1er is filled with trees and plants imported from all corners of the world. It stands on the spot where the

Paillon River used to pour into the Mediterranean. Most of the Paillon has been covered over, to make way for roads, gardens, fountains and major public buildings, in a very successful feat of urban planning. But if you look at the map, you can easily see where it used to flow, and how it cut Nice in two. On the one side (to the east), the old town and the port; on the other side, what is now the commercial centre of the town, on both sides of **avenue Jean Médecin** which starts at **Place Masséna**, with its lovely deep-red facades (the architect, Vernier, also designed the Rue de Rivoli in Paris).

At carnival-time (around February), this is the centre of the action, and the buildings are covered with the grotesque characters that have made the Nice carnival so famous. At the bottom end of the avenue are the big shops and department-stores, and in the side-streets, (**rue Gioffredo**, **rue Hôtel des Postes**, and **rue de France**), the smaller shops which may have just the thing you've always wanted. If it's especially hot, walk into **Nice Etoile**, the super-modern air-conditioned shopping-mall on avenue Médecin. (The **Espace Niçoise d'Art et de Culture** on the third floor often shows the work of *Niçois* artists).

On the other side of the Paillon, there is *Le Vieux Nice* (the old town). From the **Place Masséna**, you step down into the narrow streets, which become narrower and darker the further in you go. The shady doorways, and the cramped little shops are particularly striking if you have just come off the beach, still blinded by the sun. Hidden away in its mysterious corners are art-galleries, artisans and artists. In the **rue de la Poissonnerie** (n° 2), the huge but gentle Yugoslav painter Slobodan will talk to you about the little smiling men in hats which haunt his naïve paintings, then you can visit the ateliers of Sosno, Asselot, and other rising stars of the *Niçois* art-world. Art has an important place in the life of this neighbourhood. After the shops have closed, you can admire the work of local painters who have decorated their metal shutters — just one example of the happenings organised by internationally-known artists. In a more conventional but equally artistic vein, there are two art-galleries on the **Quai des Etats Unis** (sea-front of the old town), the **Galerie des Ponchettes** and the **Galérie d'Art Contemporain**, which show the work of greater — and lesser — modern artists.

The other striking feature of the old town is the food: bakeries, groceries, delicatessens and restaurants, their offerings spilling out into the streets. Specialities of Nice include tiny black olives, many varieties of fresh pasta, huge *pans bagnats* (traditional sandwiches) and assorted vegetable-pies. Squeezed in between the food-shops are some of the smartest (and cheapest) clothing stores of the Riviera. Shopkeepers and customers jostle each other in the narrow streets, joking and laughing, often speaking to each other in *Niçois*, the original language of the *Comté de Nice*.

Between the old town and the sea, the **Cours Saleya**, recently renovated, is the largest market of fruit, vegetables and flowers in the region: a wonderful splash of colour in the Mediterranean sunlight. In early summer, you can fill your hotel room with flowers for the price of a meal. Prices are clearly displayed and *you* decide which product to buy. Look for the the label *pays* (pronounced 'payee'), which tells you that the produce is locally grown. Note that there is no market on Mondays, and that in the afternoons, the cafés spread out their tables under the market-awnings. Have a *pastis*, and watch the world go by. For lunch or dinner, you can take your pick of seafood restaurants on the Cours Saleya, or risk your luck with the local cooking in the heart of the old town. On Wednesday afternoons, artists and artisans display their craft.

Back to the Paillon, and this time follow the avenue "upstream" to high-tech country — the **Acropolis**, a mammoth conference centre, with endless levels and staircases and halls, in shimmering glass and steel, surrounded by fountains and sculpture. Built to attract international meetings and conferences, it seems to be taking off in a big way, housing the *Cinémathèque* of Nice and playing host to a large number of cultural events and major exhibitions.

Finally, for yet another change of pace, drive or take a bus up the hill to **Cimiez**, and drift back into the *grande époque* of the Riviera, among the gardens and stately mansions that gaze serenely down onto the city. Cimiez was once a centre for noble and wealthy tourists, and the hotels of the epoch can still be seen and admired: the **Winter Palace**, the **Regina Palace**, the **Hermitage**, the **Alhambra**, the **Carlton**, the **Imperial**. Palms and bougainvillea, neatly trimmed lawns and quiet streets. In a sense, we have come full circle — from the dream-world of sugar-icing palaces of the Promenade des Anglais, to the decayed splendour of Cimiez. But between the two lie the busy, breathless rush of central Nice, the picturesque old town with its crafts and markets, and the space-craft shape of the Acropolis — proof that the city of Nice will still be alive and well for many years to come.

WHERE TO STAY IN NICE

Nice has a long tradition of high-class hotel service with an extensive choice in all categories. If you arrive without a reservation and have no friends to drop in on (ill-advised in the height of summer or at carnaval-time), you may want to get in touch with the tourist board, the *Syndicat d'Initiative* (Tel: 93.87.07.07 or 93.87.60.60) where people are extremely courteous and helpful. They can put you touch with hotels located in the area you prefer.

If money is no object, you will probably gravitate towards the **Promenade des Anglais**, where the more royal suites can cost you several thousand francs a day. To our knowledge, only one hotel on the Promenade sinks as low as two-stars (and it's not on our recommended list!). If you're in the two- and three-star market, **avenue Maréchal-Joffre** and **boulevard Victor-Hugo**, a little further inland, (but still only a few minutes' walk from the beach) are better bets.

One word of warning: central Nice is not renowned for peace and quiet, and, if this is important for you, check which way your room faces, especially if you are staying near the centre. In some areas, the morning markets get going just about the time the last revellers are straggling home from the discos.

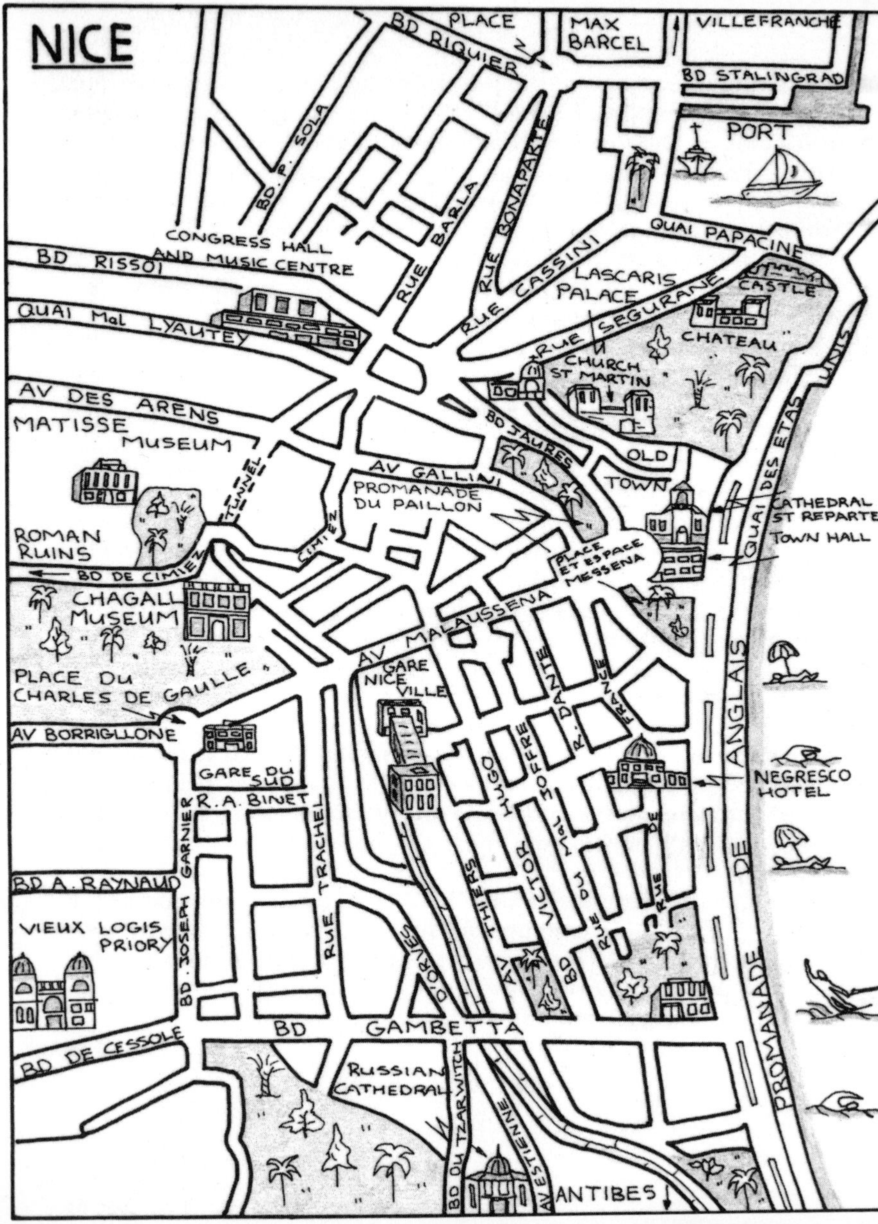
NICE
PLACE
MAX BARCEL
VILLEFRANCHE
BD RIQUIER
BD STALINGRAD
PORT
BD. P. SOLA
RUE BARLA
RUE BONAPARTE
QUAI PAPACINE
CONGRESS HALL AND MUSIC CENTRE
BD RISSOI
RUE CASSINI
LASCARIS PALACE
CASTLE
QUAI Mal LYAUTEY
RUE SEGURANE
CHATEAU
CHURCH ST MARTIN
AV DES ARENS
MATISSE MUSEUM
BD JAURES
OLD TOWN
TUNNEL
AV GALLINI
PROMANADE DU PAILLON
QUAI DES ETATS UNIS
CATHEDRAL ST REPARTE
TOWN HALL
ROMAN RUINS
CIMIEZ
PLACE ET ESPACE MESSENA
BD DE CIMIEZ
CHAGALL MUSEUM
AV MALAUSSENA
PLACE DU CHARLES DE GAULLE
GARE NICE VILLE
R. DANTE
FRANCE
AV BORRIGLLONE
GARE DU SUD
HUGO
Mal JOFFRE
NEGRESCO HOTEL
R.A. BINET
BD JOSEPH GARNIER
RUE TRACHEL
BD A. RAYNAUD
VIEUX LOGIS PRIORY
AV THIERS
BD VICTOR
RUE DU
RUE DE
D'ORVES
BD GAMBETTA
BD DE CESSOLE
RUSSIAN CATHEDRAL
BD DU TZARWITCH
AV ESTIENNE
ANTIBES
PROMANADE DE ANGLAIS

CREME DE LA CREME

NEGRESCO
Promenade des Anglais (next to Musée Masséna)
Tel: 93.88.39.51

Declared a historic monument in 1974, and if you dream of exiled Russian princes drinking champagne out of lady's slippers after losing everything on one spin of a roulette-wheel, this is the place for you. The white, black and gold facade, the works of art on the walls, the superb restaurant (the **Chantecler**) and royal service, are all features that many hotels would like to be able to imitate. Rooms start at about 1000 F.

BEACH REGENCY
223, Promenade des Anglais
Tel: 93.83.91.51

Close to the airport near the end of the Promenade, the ex-Hyatt Regency, taken over by the **Abéla** group, this is luxury at the more modern end of the scale. Not much romance, but plenty of comfort in these spacious rooms, with large terraces, video and air-conditioning. Swimming-pool on the roof, sauna, piano-bar, boutiques... From 500 to 1000 F.

MERIDIEN
1, Promenade des Anglais
Tel: 93.82.25.25

Couldn't be more central and still be on the Promenade (opposite end to the Beach Regency). This modern luxury hotel has acquired a reputation for excellent and friendly service, remarkable for a hotel catering mainly to the business-traveller (albeit the well-heeled). Heated pool, air-conditioning, and lots of other services. Rates start at around 500 F and go up and up.

WESTMINSTER CONCORDE
27, Promenade des Anglais
Tel: 93.88.29.44

Closer to the Negresco than the Méridien, both geographically and in style, and a good place to stay for night-birds interested in exploring the town. Old-style service, well-preserved, but with plenty of modern conveniences, including its own disco. From 500 to 900 F.

LESS EXTRAVAGANT

LA MALMAISON (3*)
48, boulevard Victor-Hugo
Tel: 93.87.62.56

Traditional-style decoration in beautiful high-ceilinged rooms, with balconies and pleasant, low-key service. Central. From 280 to 400 F.

VICTORIA (3*)
33, boulevard Victor-Hugo
Tel: 93.88.39.60

Just down the road from the Malmaison, another very pleasant hotel, with a lovely shady garden. Between 250 and 350 F.

LA PEROUSE
11, quai Rauba-Capeu
Tel: 93.62.34.63

Had to be mentioned because of its unique position. Unparalleled view of the bay and the long sweep of the *Promenade*. Very comfortable. Although recently, the quality of service has seriously declined. From 350 to 850 F.

BUSBY
36, rue du Maréchal Joffre.
Tel: 93.88.19.41

A friendly, family-type atmosphere. Central. Ask for rooms on the garden side. 190 to 300 F.

HOTEL GEORGES
3, rue Henri Cordier
Tel: 93.86.23.41

Not particularly close to the centre (accessible by bus), but close to the sea, a very pleasant, clean hotel, with helpful staff.
From 180 F.

IBIS
47, blvd Corniglion-Molinier
Tel: 93. 83.30.30

If you're just here for a night or two or need to be close to the airport, this hotel has comfortable but standardised rooms at reasonable prices starting around 250 F.

HOLIDAY INN
179, blvd René-Cassin
Tel: 93.83.91.92

Just up the road from the airport, with even more comfortable rooms than the Ibis (but just as standardised), at less reasonable prices beginning at around 500 F.

THE BEACHES AND THE SEA

No one looking for a beach to spend the day on would deliberately go to Nice. There is a lovely view of the **Baie des Anges**, but the beaches are pebbly and rather steep. For this very reason, they are not as over-crowded as you might expect.

On the other hand, if you are in Nice for some other reason, it's good to know you can go for a swim any time you want, and that the beaches are a few minutes walk from the centre of town.

For a quick swim, go to the public beaches (easy access down the steps from the **Promenade des Anglais**). If you are going to spend more than a few hours, however, you might prefer a private beach, where you can stretch out on a mattress, in the sun or under a parasol, and have drinks and snacks brought to you with a wave of the hand. The private beaches also rent out water-sports equipment and some have facilities for water-skiing or water-parachuting.

If you want to eat on the beach, there's **Coco Beach**, recommended in *Gault-Millau*, but even that guide for the well-heeled gourmet liked it but found the prices high. Several other beaches have restaurants, and the prices are not always excessive. For elegance and comfort, away from the crowds, choose the **Neptune** beach (with a sauna). For atmosphere, the **Plage de L'Opéra**, up at the eastern end, and for maritime sports and boating, the **Lido Plage** or **Gallus 80**, near the big hotels.

However, if you're looking for good seafood, you'd better go around the other side of the *Colline du Château* and eat on the port.The harbour is nice to look at on a sunny day, and a meal on the terrace of **Le Chalutier** or at the **Ane Rouge** is probably the best way to get to know it. (Both on the Quai des Deux Emmanuels, telephone respectively, 93.98.58.05 and 93.89.49.63). See the restaurant chapter for further listings.

Nice has practically no facilities for pleasure-boats. Yachtsmen will put in at other points down the coast — Antibes, Monaco and the new port of Saint Laurent. The port of Nice is used by the fishing fleet, a few cargo vessels, and the **ferry** to Corsica (a 6-to-7 hour crossing, daily departures in high season).

A WALK ON THE SUNNY SIDE OF HISTORY

Throughout history, a lot of people have thought of Nice as a pretty good place to settle. Four hundred thousand years ago, when sabre-toothed tigers and mammoths still wandered around without a leash, cavemen and women were setting up cave in this very spot.

Later generations agreed that the location of Nice had a lot to be said for it. However, they were no longer living in the rocks, and preferred to hang out in temples, castles, palaces, casinos, luxury hotels, or even shopping arcades, depending on the taste of the century. The final result of their habitations, worshipping-haunts and eating-places is Nice as it is today, a delightful hodge-podge of history, and still a pretty good place to settle.

Some guides suggest that you can visit Nice more or less in the order it was settled, starting with the cavemen, and ending in the 20th century. We have found, however, that whichever period of Nice you want to look at, some other century keeps getting in the way, and confusing the issue. So perhaps the best way is just to wander around history, without caring too much about rigour and scholarship.

The Port: Prehistory

Apparently, the first humans to make fire made it right here, which is rather surprising. We had always imagined that fire was the discovery of prehistoric Danes or Britons trying to warm up draughty caves. On a warm summer night overlooking the *Baie des Anges*, a caveman might be tempted to say, "Why bother?" (It was a long and tedious business in those days). On the other hand, perhaps they were having winters like those of '84 and '85 (which killed off all the palm trees), when even the toughest of cavemen would have been feeling the cold.

You can find the answer to any questions you might have about cavemen at the **Terra Amata Museum** (25, boulevard Carnot, Tel: 93.55.59.93) where you can see an actual prehistoric dwelling, fully-furnished, on the site where it was found. This museum of prehistory is designed to interest even those who think that prehistory is a bore. Explanations in English, and lots of fun exhibits with lights and voices. Located two minutes from the port, and within walking-distance of at least six excellent seafood restaurants (see section on "Beaches and the Sea", or the chapter on **Eating Out**).

La Colline du Château

The *Château* of Nice is a bad joke: there *is* no *Château*. Tourists can spend a long time hunting around on the hill before learning that it was pulled down in 1706 to be replaced by gardens and fountains. Breathe a sigh of relief — there's nothing you really have to visit up here except a little **Naval Museum** (for enthusiasts only). Have a drink under the trees — one of the coolest, pleasantest places to spend a hot summer afternoon.

At the time of the cavemen, this hill was an island and present-day Nice was at the bottom of a big bay. You can walk all around this ex-island, and look down on the neighbourhoods you're going to visit next.

THE OLD CITY: FROM THE GREEKS TO THE AVANT-GARDE

The Greeks founded Nice (called Nikaïa at the time) at the top of Castle Hill. Several centuries later, it got crowded, and people started moving down the west side of the hill. This triangular area, between the hill and the Paillon River (now covered over) is called *Le Vieux Nice* or *La Vieille Ville*, famous for lovely buildings, little bistros, shops and avant-garde artists.

A lot of the buildings are baroque, including most of the churches. Church-crawlers will have a field-day: there are **seven** baroque churches or chapels within a few hundred yards of each other (look at any city map). More interesting to the average visitor, however, is the **Palais Lascaris**, a 17th-century building, completely restored and magnificently furnished, with an 18th-century pharmacy on the ground floor. The *Palais* is also a **Museum of Popular Arts and Traditions** which organises walks around the old city (recommended) and is a major source of information for visitors.

A Touch of Gastronomy and Fashion

A more fattening way of exploring the old city is in search of traditional *Niçois* cuisine. Don't leave before trying some *socca* (a kind of chick-pea pancake), *tourte de blettes, ravioli niçois, soupe au pistou* (made with basil), or even *stockfisch,* a bizarre stew made of dried fish imported from Scandinavia — a dish invented in the nineteenth century by a *restaurateur* left with several tons of dried fish he couldn't sell. The best addresses for eating *niçois* are **Lou Balico** (20, avenue Saint Jean Baptiste, Tel: 93.85.93.71), where the now legendary Adrienne rules behind the cauldrons and **Nissa-Socca** (5, rue Sainte Réparate, Tel: 93.80.18.35). See also the chapter on **Eating Out**.

More and more shops open every year in the little back-streets of the old city, many of them selling articles by inventive young designers of Nice. Some of best young artists of modern France have their *ateliers* here. The *Ecole de Nice* was born in the *Vieille Ville* . You can also see the *tôle-art,* paintings by well-known artists on the old metal shutters of the shops. On and around the **Cours Saleya** (the flower market), you can buy elegant and inventive clothes for very reasonable prices (much cheaper than in Juan-les-Pins).

Cimiez:
Jazz Amidst the Ruins

On the big hill north of central Nice is where the Romans settled and where you find all the ruins — the **Roman Arena** and the **Forum** (with temples and villas). There is also an **Archaeological Museum** (164, avenue des Arènes-de-Cimez, Tel: 93.81.59.57) displaying the jewelry, pottery and statues found here.

Nowadays, the Arena is the scene of a number of events, the most famous being the **Grande Parade de Jazz** in July, which assembles numerous world-famous artists to play in the Roman amphitheatre and among the olive trees surrounding it. At other times of year, the Cimiez Jazz Club also invites interesting artists.

Musée Matisse, in the same building as the Archaeological Museum (same phone number) has a lot of the canvases showing scenes of the region.

Modern Nice

Long after you have forgotten the museums, the beaches, the shops and the nighclubs, you will remember the boulevards and avenues of Nice, the white wedding-cake hotels and the terra-cotta pink-and-ochre houses. The best way to see them is from an open-top sports car on a clear sunny day, when the traffic is light (a tip: in summer, drive around between 1 and 3 pm). On the **Promenade des Anglais**, for example, you will drive past the **Hotel Negresco**, with its lackeys in livery, the **Musée Masséna** (right next door) fronted by an elegant garden, the sad, closed-up **Palais de la Méditerranée** casino (victim of the bloody Casino Wars of the late 70's), and many other anonymous, strangely decorated, nineteenth century mansions.

Little by little, to save space, they are bricking over the bed of the Paillon River (actually, a bit of an exaggeration for this dried-up trickle). It is being replaced with gardens, a disguised bus-station and big municipal buildings. From the **Place Masséna**, you can walk south through the **Jardins Albert 1er** to the sea, or north through a series of plazas with dramatic fountains. The success of this transformation has prompted the opening of a series of busy new cafés and restaurants. Still further north, past the **Theatre** (which often puts on musical or dance shows), you come to the impressive **Acropolis Conference Centre**. Feel free to go in, to get information at the desk (in particular, the calender of events), and to wander around.

Another example of modern architecture in Nice is the **Nice-Etoile** shopping mall (avenue Jean Médecin) which has become very popular for elegant shopping at sensible prices.

PLEASANT WAYS TO WATCH THE WORLD GO BY

Nice is a city of action and energy. The *Niçois* go into cafés to argue, do business and discuss the ways of the world — all serious activities, accomplished with much movement and many gestures. *Boules*, which is played in every street and backyard of the Riviera, may seem like an idle pastime, but is played with concentration and passion.

The visitor, however, is here to relax and observe. One of the great pleasures of a Mediterranean city is the opportunity offered just to sit and watch. Here are some suggestions.

LE GRAND CAFE DE TURIN

5, place Garibaldi
Tel: 93.62.29.52

Whole volumes could be written about this café, an oyster-bistrot in the old tradition, and a legend in the history of old Nice. In its dusty halls, you can watch *Niçois* society of all classes and ages come and go.

THE SCOTCH TEA HOUSE

4, avenue de Suède et Gustave-V
(opposite the Jardin Albert 1er)
Tel: 93.87.75.62

A totally different tradition of the Riviera is that of the tea-houses – introduced by the English, of course, and still very *olde England*, but at the same time quite unlike anything British. They can be elegant, and even fashionable. This one is a hang-out of the famous sculptor, César.

BAR OF THE NEGRESCO

37, Promenade des Anglais
Tel: 93.88.39.51

A variant of the tea-houses, this represents the international and ageless elegance of Nice, and everyone should have a drink here once. No need to stay long however: "action" is not the word to describe what's going on.

PROMENADE DES ANGLAIS

While on the Promenade, just pull over, park your car (easier said than done) and wander up and down a little. Sit down on a bench or a balustrade and watch them all go by: the very genteel in discreet but expensive clothes; the old ladies, all with a dog in tow; the *branchés*, with died hair and black make-up; the naked (or almost) flexing their muscles or curving their curves as they drift on and off the beaches; a bus-load of tourists *en route* for another site; roller-skaters rolling, joggers jogging, and back-packers hefting their packs; the very rich and the totally destitute. The endless, endlessly fascinating show of the Riviera.

LE FLORE
Place Magenta
(in the pedestrian area)

The pedestrian streets, and in particular **rue Masséna** and **Place Magenta** are favourite hang-outs in summer, when the cheap restaurants and the cafés spread their tables out in the open air. An easy place to meet people and chat. Close to the centre and the shops.

LES PONCHETTES
Cours Saleya
Old town

A trendy clientele and very full in summer. The nearby street-market provides a colourful backdrop to all that's going on here. Plenty of tourists, but also plenty of *Niçois*, coming out of the backwoods of the *Vieille Ville* to see what's going on in the wide world. A good stop-off point if you're shopping in this area.

SOMETHING TO TAKE HOME

As the capital of the entire Riviera region, Nice provides all the hustle and bustle of a major town. Its shopping facilities cater to all tastes — from punk to *mesdames*. The main shopping centre radiates around the **avenue Jean Médecin**, offering big department stores such as the **Nouvelles Galeries** and the modern centre of **Nice-Etoile**, plus the lively pedestrian area of **rue Masséna**. Name designers and more expensive boutiques are to be found in **avenue de Suède** and **rue Paradis**, opposite the Albert 1er Gardens. **Rue de la Liberté**, running parallel to rue Masséna, and **rue Longchamp** just next-door also have some classy little shops. For younger trendier styles, try the boutiques around the **Cours Saleya**, and in the picturesque streets of the *Vielle Ville* .

Real shopping fanatics can also make a day of it at the huge shopping centre **Cap 3000**, just beyond Nice Airport. This indoor complex on two levels accommodates all types of boutiques, a big department store and supermarket, plus cafés and restaurants for when you collapse.

WOMEN'S FASHIONS

JEAN-LOUIS SCHERRER
4, avenue de Suède
Tel: 93.87.88.29

A classic designer with an infallible sense for style and sheer femininity.

GLADYS FALK
2, rue Paradis
Tel: 93.82.06.48

Stocks a selection of well-known labels including **Montana, Giorgio Armani, Comme Les Garçons, Tarlazzi** and leatherwear by **Alaïa**. Prices predictably steep.

GIGI
10, rue de la Liberté
Tel: 93.87.81.78

One of the most popular boutiques in Nice with a great variety of avant-garde designers – **Emmanuel Kahn, Yamamoto, Thierry Mugler, Enrico Coveri, Byblos, Anne-Marie Beretta, Chantal Thomass**... Non-pushy service.

MISS KENZO
21, rue du Marché
Old Town
Tel: 93.85.51.56

For the young crowd, but still with the emphasis on name designers (except Kenzo!) – with consequently high prices: **Georges Rech, J.-P. Gaultier, Iceberg (Castelbajac**'s Italian range).

VERTIGE
11bis, rue Maréchal Joffre
Tel: 93.87.88.71

Where to buy that sexy French underwear you've always dreamed of, with classy labels such as **Pascale Madonna, Anabelle** and **Valentino**.

STEPHANE KELIAN
8, rue Alphonse Karr
Tel: 93.82.28.81

The most exquisite shoes and sandals – but be prepared for exceptional prices (900-1200 F for this year's two-tone sandals).

LES HALLES – KILIWATCH
39, rue de la Préfecture
Tel: 93.80.67.99

For guys and gals looking for something a bit different – meaning retro styles from the fifties and sixties. Gabardine trousers, sexy dresses, tuxedoes, trench-coats – all at fairly reasonable prices, plus a big stock of *fripes* (2nd hand).

MENS FASHIONS

BOOMERANG
1, rue Longchamp
Tel: 93.81.76.25

For casual elegance and original designs by **Mugler, Gaulthier, Castelbajac** and **Gerbaud**.

LACOSTE
6, avenue de Suède
Tel. 93.87.75.45

The full range of classic French sportswear with the ubiquitous crocodile logo.

FACONNABLE
7-9, rue Paradis
Tel: 93.87.88.80

A successful line of smart but casual clothes well-suited to the Mediterranean life-style.

TRABAUD
10, rue de la Liberté
Tel: 93.87.53.96

Cool Italian suits in fine cotton fabrics or linen, signed **Cerruti** or **Valentino**, to knock 'em dead back in Ohio! Provided, of course, that your pocketbook can sustain the shock.

KIDS' GEAR

AMERICAN GRAFFITI
Nice-Etoile
Tel: 93.85.85.11
Cap 3000
Tel: 93.29.40.50

For youngsters with hyped-up clothes sense – the latest in **Liberto** jeans, the **Fiorucci** collection, **Chevignon** leather- wear, **Chipie**, **Taverniti**, etc...

ANNIE FRAMBOISE
1, rue Longchamp
Tel: 93.87.98.97

Classic (and expensive) clothes for the little darlings, plus the latest from **Taverniti**, **Closed**, **Va Bene**, **Liberto** for trendy kids up to age 14.

JEWELLERS

HUART
6, rue Paradis
Tel: 93.87.23.23

Selection of prestigious names including jewellery by **Chopard** and **Van Cleef and Arpels, Must de Cartier**, **Dupont** lighters and **Morabito** luggage. French watches bearing the **Hublot** and **Concord** labels.

NEREIDES
12, rue Paradis
Tel: 93.82.18.00

Fun jewelry in a pretty shop with brassy bangles, ear-rings, bracelets etc. plus a more expensive line in gold and silver.

LUGGAGE AND HOME DECORATION

LOUIS VUITTON
2, avenue de Suède
Tel: 93.87.87.47

For those who can't resist its

ubiquitous logo – the full range of high-quality luggage and accessories.

PECHA
3, place Masséna
Tel: 93.53.48.68

Something truly (and expensively) French for the home – tableware by **Christofle, Baccarat, Lalique**, etc.

THE ART MART

FERRERO
24, rue de France
Tel: 93.88.34.44

A very wide selection of prints and lithographs (from 500 F) by modern masters such as **Dali, Picasso, Chagall, Miro, Cocteau, César** etc. A signed litho by **Chagall** or **Picasso** will set you back around 20,000 F.

SAPONE
25, boulevard Victor Hugo
Tel: 93.88.54.27

The best gallery in Nice for contemporary art. Permanent collection plus individual exhibitions (eg. **Picasso** sculptures 1930-1960 from May 30 to July 31).

VILLAGE SEGURANE
off rue Catherine Ségurane

An indoor maze of antique shops with some interesting items but very few bargains.

LES PUCES
(Flea-Market)
Boulevard Risso

Near Nice's theatre – an outdoor flea-market with the usual bric-à-brac, where you might find the perfect souvenir to take back home.

FOR GOURMETS

COMTESSE DU BARRY
5, rue Halévy
Tel: 93.88.49.16

Specialties from the southwest of France such as *foie gras*, plus wines and spirits.

HEDIARD
Cap 3000
Tel: 93.31.56.04

The famous Parisian store that has supplied fine food fans with the best in groceries, herbal teas, wines, spirits, etc. for the last 130 years.

EXCURSIONS FROM NICE

Westward

If you head westwards from Nice, you cross the Var river and come to **Saint Laurent**, cut in half by the autoroute, and buried in unattractive housing-developments dating from the 50's and 60's. It's sad, because the **old town** is very charming, if you can find your way to through the high-rise buildings and the road-junctions.

On the other side of the autoroute, close to the big, elegant shopping mall of **Cap 3000**, there is the **Port of Saint Laurent**, a pleasure-boat harbour that has taken off in a big way, and is becoming a fashionable spot to drink and dine.

West and North of Saint Laurent, we come to the region described in full in the chapter, **The Heart of the Riviera.**

Northward into the Alps

Northwards, up the east bank of the Var, you are very soon in the foothills of the Alps, what the *Niçois* call *les vallées*, a wild and beautiful region, but no longer the Riviera, and too big to be properly covered by this guide. Lovers of dramatic alpine scenery will take trips up the narrow mountain roads, past the tiny villages perched on impossible peaks of rock, and stop to eat fresh trout or game in simple country inns.

Hikers and nature-lovers will drive up the **Vallée de la Vésubie** (up the Vésubie river) to the **Vallée de la Gordolasque** (past **Belvedere**) or to **Saint Martin Vésubie**, the hiking capital of the southern Alps. Within a few kilometres, trails lead up towards 10,000-foot peaks, with lakes, glaciers and cascades, through the **PARC NATIONAL DU MERCANTOUR**. Detailed information about the Park can be obtained from any tourist-office.

Saint Martin has a number of hotels (book well in advance for

TOURISTOR

the summer season), or you can stay in any of the towns or villages on the way up. The town of **Lantosque**, an otherwise rather gloomy place with dark slate roofs, has one of the nicest modest-priced hotels in the whole Riviera area, **L'Ancienne Gendarmerie** (06450 Lantosque, Tel: 93.03.00.65), overlooking the river. The restaurant, run by young master Solveig, has a menu at 103 F which could easily cost twice as much down on the coast.

Skiers will also become familiar with these valleys, but they will tend to choose the **Vallée de la Tinée** or the **Gorges du Cians**, where they will find the three biggest ski-resorts within easy access of the coast: **ISOLA 2000** *(Maison d'Isola,* Tel: 93.23.10.50, Telex 461 666) is so named because the lowest slopes are 2000 metres above sea-level. It is a well-equipped modern resort, a little too like a busy railway-station for some people's liking; **AURON** (Tel: 93.23.02.66, Telex 470 300 F) is at a lower altitude, but has the best restaurants and night-life; **VALBERG** (Tel 93.02.52.54) is a family resort set in the middle of forests, with fewer slopes than Isola or Auron, but more varied scenery. All three are proud of the high sunshine-rate of their resorts, and Isola even offers a special ski-pass which gives you a week's free skiing if there is no sun for three days! Detailed information on prices and accomodation can be obtained by writing to the **Syndicat d'Initiative** of each resort.

Northwest to Peille and Peillon

The two villages of **Peille** and **Peillon** can be reached either by driving northwards out of central Nice, through La Trinité and Drap, the ugly suburbs running alongside the Paillon River (Take the D2204, then turn right on the D21), or else by taking the autoroute to La Turbie, and taking the D53, to reach Peille from the other end.

PEILLON is famous for its village architecture. It is built on a rocky spur, where many would find it difficult to place a single house. As a result, the houses are placed almost on top of each other, and linked by bridges which criss-cross over the narrow streets. Not to be outdone, **PEILLE** calls itself the "most unusual village of the Alpes Maritimes", an ambitious claim, because many of these little villages have some very strange features. In any case, you can spend an interesting couple of hours exploring its corners and covered streets.

Between the two villages, there is lovely countryside, with places to picnic and walk. Hikers may be tempted by the trail which goes from the ruined **Château of Drap** (on the hill above **Chateauvieux**) past the pilgrimage spot of **Notre Dame de Laghet**, then on to Peille and Peillon.

David Ward-Perkins, Editor and Jill Harry

JILL HARRY is a free-lance writer, editor and translator who has been living in the South of France for the last five years.

4
THE HEART OF THE RIVIERA:

ANTIBES,
JUAN-LES-PINS,
CAGNES-SUR-MER,
VENCE AND ST. PAUL

84 | The Heart of the Riviera
86 | Where to Stay
89 | Interesting Things To Do
93 | The Beaches and the Sea
95 | Hanging Around
98 | Something to Take Home

HEART OF THE RIVIERA

When the great artists of the late 19th and early 20th century — Renoir, Miro, Picasso, Matisse — came to live on the Riviera, they chose neither Nice nor Cannes, but settled in the countryside between, in the towns and villages and farms which make up the heart of the Riviera.

Renoir chose **Cagnes-sur-Mer**, living out his last days in a bucolic setting among the olive trees, painting the rounded limbs and sweet smiles of local maidens. Not long after his death, in the old town of Cagnes — the **Haut de Cagnes** — a noisier breed of artists celebrated the 20's, under the aegis of the extraordinary Suzy Solidor. Inside the **Château**, you will find several dozen portraits of Suzy, painted by the hand of the greatest artists and illustrators of the time, including Dali, Utrillo, Cocteau and Van Dongen. Several look like they were painted in the early hours of the morning, with the festivities still going strong. Suzy Solidor's antique store is still open today, and at night, the narrow streets of the *haut de Cagnes* are still cluttered with revellers' sports-cars. There are discothèques and night-clubs (not always heterosexual) on the **Place du Château**, and in the **Montée de La Bourgade**, just behind the castle, you can eat in the little restaurants where today's artists go to meet and celebrate.

Further up the valley of the River Cagne, artists behave with more poise and discretion, as witnessed by the **Chapelle de la Rosaire** in **Vence**, decorated by Matisse and a masterpiece of good taste. Vence is very attractive, and very sedate. It has a few quiet hotels, some friendly shop-keepers and no nightlife of any kind. People come here to rest or to retire.

Vence is also the gateway to the mountain-country. On the slopes behind, you can hear the sound of sheep-bells, and see the last line of houses marking the boundary of the *Côte d'Azur* and the *arrière-pays*, the dry, wild landscapes of the back-country. A few kilometers away, the little villages of **Tourettes-sur-Loup** and **Saint Jeannet** cling precariously to the slopes. Tourettes is a centre for crafts, and both villages are the home of artists —

anonymous painters, sculptors and writers who live and mix with the farmers of the region.

A few kilometers down the road, back towards the coast, the village of **Saint Paul-de-Vence** is anything but anonymous. A constant flow of visitors pours from the cars and tourist coaches into the village made famous by Cocteau, Chagall, Prévert, Giacometti, and a hundred other artists and intellectuals. In Saint Paul, everyone is more famous than everyone else. As you sit at the **Café de la Place**, with its high ceilings and marble tables, the two men playing *boules* with the locals on the square may be film-stars Yves Montand and Lino Ventura. The conversation at the next table may include writer James Baldwin, and the familiar face you see in the car driving by may be musician Bill Wyman of the Rolling Stones, or Roger Moore, both of whom live just outside the village.

Great names of art and entertainment have chosen to live in the heart of the Riviera for generations, not only for the gentle beauty of its woods and valleys, now covered in villas, but also for the simple welcome that the villagers have always given to foreigners. In this part of the world, a *pastis* and a chat is an obligatory introduction to any form of business. In Saint Paul, in spite of the tourists and the exposure, the strongest lobby in the Town Hall is that of the farmers — and that's the way everyone wants it.

In **Antibes**, which includes the sparkling beach-resort of **Juan-les-Pins**, the biggest industry isn't tourism. It's flowers. As you fly into Nice-Côte d'Azur airport over Antibes, you can see the rows and rows of greenhouses from the air. The symbol of Antibes is a rose, and the biggest and oldest families of the city are the growers. Picasso lived here, before he moved up the hill to **Vallauris**. His paintings and pottery in the **Picasso Museum** (in the **Château d'Antibes**), indicate that he was living life very much to the full in spite of his advancing years.

Many others have settled here by the sea, including novelist Graham Greene, who still lives in an apartment close to the **Port of Antibes** — the biggest pleasure-boat harbour in the world, where the yachts of the very rich tower over the tiny fishing-fleet which still brings in the day's catch for the local restaurants.

Nowadays, some of the quay-side restaurants are rumoured to be serving frozen fish, and some of the paintings sold on café terraces by art-students are really mass-produced in Taiwan. But nobody is seriously worried. Discerning travellers will know the difference, and look beyond the surface. In this heartland of the Riviera, even in the summer rush, foreigners will be welcomed, as the artists of the world before them, with warmth and understanding.

WHERE TO STAY

There are few famous hotels between Cannes and Nice, and for the well-heeled traveller there is not a great choice. For the less wealthy, however, there are modest hotels with a pleasant family feeling, set in some of the nicest locations of the Riviera.

The quality you get for the price you pay is often higher the further you go from the coast, and **Vence** may not be a bad place to choose as a base. It's less than twenty minutes from the sea, and gets pleasant cool breezes in summer, as well as being considerably calmer and more relaxing than a resort like Juan-les-Pins. Ten minutes from Vence, you can get onto the *autoroute* which will take you to any part of the Riviera, so, in a sense, Vence is even more central than Nice or Cannes.

If you are staying any length of time, try and rent a villa or apartment (the **John Taylor** agency is one of the biggest, with offices all down the coast). Be aware, however, that prices for summer rental can be extremely high, and that you are unlikely to find anything if you wait until the last minute.

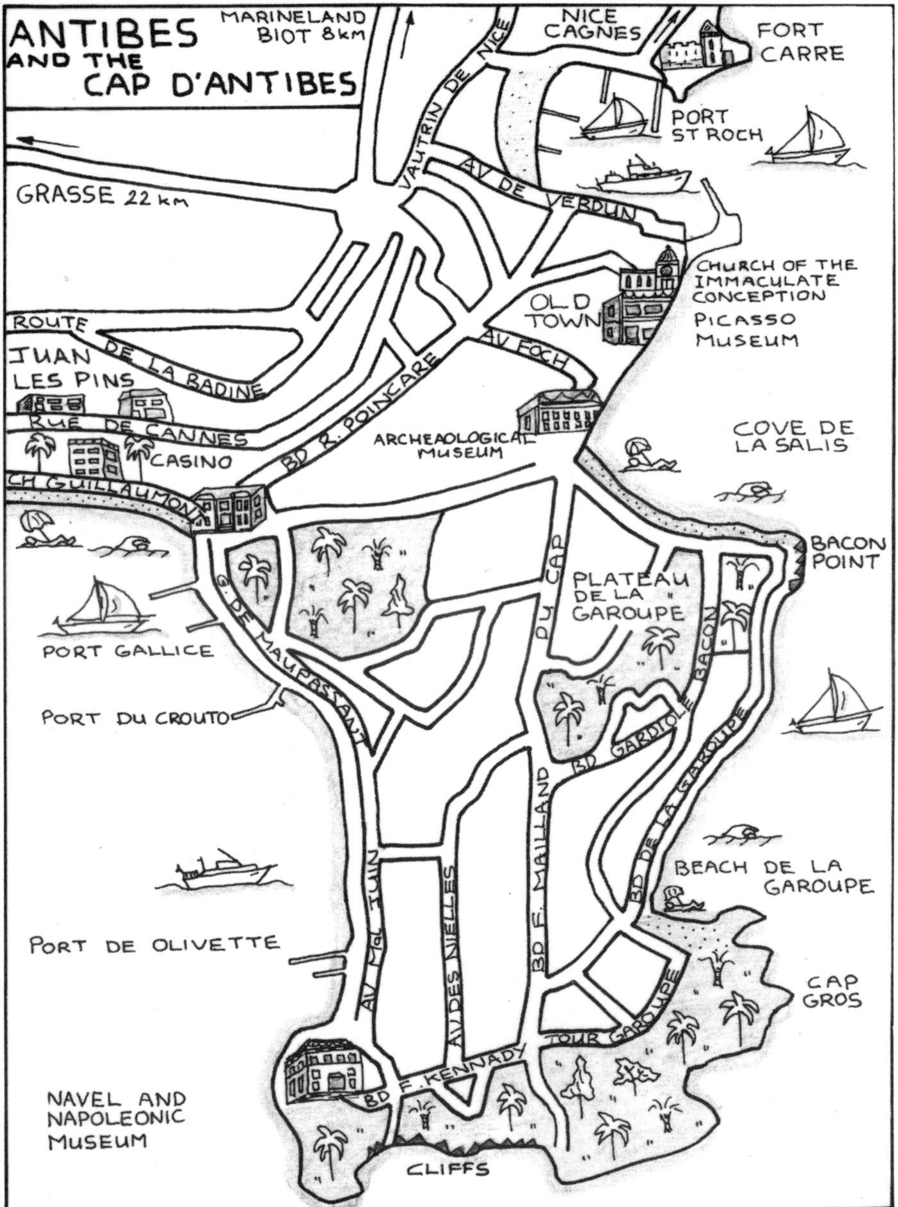
ANTIBES
AND THE
CAP D'ANTIBES
MARINELAND
BIOT 8km
NICE
CAGNES
FORT
CARRE
VAUTRIN DE NICE
PORT
ST ROCH
GRASSE 22 km
AV DE VERDUN
CHURCH OF THE
IMMACULATE
CONCEPTION
PICASSO
MUSEUM
OLD
TOWN
ROUTE DE LA BADINE
AV FOCH
JUAN
LES PINS
BD R. POINCARE
RUE DE CANNES
ARCHEAOLOGICAL
MUSEUM
COVE DE
LA SALIS
CASINO
CH GUILLAUMONT
BACON
POINT
PLATEAU
DE LA
GAROUPE
DU CAP
BACON
G. DE MAUPASSANT
PORT GALLICE
PORT DU CROUTO
BD GARDIOL
BD DE LA GAROUPE
BD F. MAILLAND
AV Mal JUIN
AV DES NIELLES
BEACH DE LA
GAROUPE
PORT DE OLIVETTE
CAP
GROS
TOUR GAROUPE
BD F. KENNADY
NAVEL AND
NAPOLEONIC
MUSEUM
CLIFFS

3 STARS and over

CHATEAU SAINT MARTIN

(4* de luxe)
Route de Coursegoules
VENCE
Tel: 93.58.02.02

Our first choice, if you can afford it (prices start at 1200 F) because of the breathtaking view, the luxurious, isolated surroundings, and the excellent restaurant (also has a pool and tennis courts).

LE MAS D'ARTIGNY

(4* de luxe)
Chemin des Salettes
SAINT-PAUL-DE-VENCE
Tel: 93.32.80.54

Even more expensive than the previous (1685 F a night), but you get an individual swimming-pool for the price!

HOTEL DU CAP

(4* de luxe)
Boulevard Kennedy
CAP D'ANTIBES
Tel: 93.61.39.01

Mentioned because of its position at the tip of the Cap d'Antibes and because it is the last of Antibes' grand hotels. The hotel and its restaurant, **Eden Roc**, are rumoured to have fallen from their former glory, and some say the prices are inflated. But anywhere on the Cap d'Antibes, if you have to ask the price, you can't afford it. (For academic interest, rooms start at 1700 F, plus 15% service charge).

HOTEL BELLES RIVES

(4* de luxe)
Bord de Mer
JUAN-LES-PINS
Tel: 93.61.02.79

If you're going to stay in Juan, you can't find a better location than this hotel, sandwiched between the sea and the *Pinède* . It doesn't have the stately calm of some other 4-star hotels, but if calm is what you want, don't stay in Juan, where the nightlife ends around breakfast-time.

LE CAGNARD

(3*)
Rue Pontis Long
HAUT DE CAGNES
Tel: 93.20.73.21

A really lovely place, in a medieval setting, in the heart of the old town. The restaurant is beginning to get an excellent reputation among connoisseurs, and the service is very charming and efficient. The hotel is small, so book well in advance. Rooms from 370 to 500 F; Suites from 650 to 900 F.

LES ORANGERS

(3*)
Route de la Colle
SAINT PAUL-DE-VENCE
Tel: 93.32.80.95

A good choice if you want to stay near Saint Paul at 3-star prices. Old-fashioned but pleasant.

1 or 2 STAR

HOTEL ASTOR

(2*)
Boulevard Poincaré (RN7)
ANTIBES
Tel: 93.61.07.38

Run by the charming Mr et Mrs Duclos, who have worked hard to make this hotel something special. Holidaymakers can rent little apartments with kitchens, and the hotel has a swimming-pool and sunning-area. The only drawback is the proximity to the road, so be sure and ask for a room giving onto the back. 330 F for a double room; 370 F for an apartment.

L'HERMITAGE

(2*)
LA GAUDE
Tel: 93.24.40.05

Something of a family hotel, in the little village of La Gaude, about ten minutes from Cagnes-sur-Mer. For those who want to taste the simpler pleasures of the Riviera. Rooms from 205 to 230 F.

AUBERGE PROVENCAL

(1*)
Place Nationale
ANTIBES
Tel: 93.34.13.24

In the very centre of Antibes, two minutes on foot from the port, the market and the Château. A very comfortable little hotel, with reasonable prices, 150 to 330 F. It has a good restaurant, and there are another ten or so within walking distance.

INTERESTING THINGS TO DO

Between the cities of Antibes and Vence, in the corridor running North to South which includes **Biot, Cagnes-sur-Mer** and **Saint Paul-de-Vence**, there are few grandiose monuments, but thousands of lovely streets and gardens. There are few miracles of nature, but a thousand beautiful views. There is little that you absolutely have to see, but a million things that catch the eye. In this heart of the French Riviera, the intelligent traveller comes as a wanderer, not as a sightseer, and takes the time to discover.

There are the traces of the great artists who have lived here.

There are the beautiful towns and villages they chose to live in. Tourists in a hurry will plan an itinerary from castle to gallery to museum and back, forgetting that the artists themselves took things more easily. Wiser visitors will leave their cars and let their instinct be their guide. They will spend time in cafés, buy fruit in markets, compare the quality of local cheeses, have lunch in back-street restaurants, and a little siesta under the olives. They will find medieval churches that are mentioned in no guide-book, and roads that appear on no map. They will never get to see some great artist's museum, but they will chat with a shop- keeper who knew the artist personally. They will **live** this wonderful region, if only for the two or three days of their stay.

THE CAP D'ANTIBES

Remember all those films set on the Riviera, in the villas of the very rich? Well, this is where they are. The Cap d'Antibes is still an exceptionally beautiful piece of coastland because of the size of some of the properties. Drive up to the lighthouse **(Phare de la Garoupe)**, and get a bird's-eye view of the Cap, and the coastline as far as Italy.

ANTIBES PROVENCAL MARKET

While the word, Provençal may bring to mind troubadours and fancy costumes, those days are long gone. However, the Provence of today is still loud, cheerful and alive. This market is held most mornings in the **Place du Marché**, the covered square in front of the *Mairie* (Town Hall). On Thursday mornings, there is also a clothes market on the **Place Nationale** just down the road, with antiques and junk for sale on the street going down to the port. Local shopkeepers join in, spreading their wares out onto the street, all traffic comes to a standstill, and the police smile helplessly from the sidelines.

While you're in the old town, you could also visit the **Château d'Antibes**, which is nice and cool in summer, and have a look at the Picasso's (Open 10 am to noon and 3 to 6 pm; closed on Tuesdays). Or just lean over the ramparts and look at the sea.

Antibes boasts the biggest pleasure-boat harbour in France. Drop in on the yacht-brokers whose offices are all around the port, and choose your next yacht.

THE POTTERIES OF VALLAURIS

This is where Picasso moved to, towards the end of his life. The pottery industry was dying, but his influence helped to revitalize the village. If you don't like pottery, don't bother to go, and if you do like pottery, be warned: the shops of Vallauris also overflow with the tasteless and the garish. You have to sift the good from the mediocre, the mediocre from the plain awful. The fun is to find the good pieces, then find out who makes them and where. Behind the flim-flam, there's a real pottery industry, with interesting things to see.

The pottery workshops are mostly on or near avenue Georges Clémenceau, the main street of Vallauris, and you don't need an appointment to go visit, as long as you go in normal business-hours. On this street you can find the *ateliers* of **Anna Camos**, and **Sassy et Milici**, two of the most famous.

A good day to go to Vallauris is Monday, market day on the **Place de l'Homme au Mouton** (named after the famous Picasso statue of a man carrying a sheep).

SOPHIA ANTIPOLIS

A rather pretentious name for one of the most famous science-parks in France, set in an idyllic site, among the pines of the **Forêt de Valbonne**. The whole project includes offices, laboratories, housing and schools, and is a flagship project for the revitalization of commerce and industry in the Southeast.

Go and take a look at it, if only to see how the planners see the Riviera of the future – a long way from beach-resorts and picture-postcard villages.

THE GLASSWORKS OF BIOT

After Vallauris, another village, another craft. The **Verreries de Biot,** Chemin des Combes, (93.65.03.00) preserve the tradition of blowing *Biot glass* , and it's worth going to see how they do it. At the end of the tour, you're led to the factory shop and expected to buy something. Why not? Some of the glass is really attractive. (Visits from Monday to Saturday, 8 am to 7 pm; Sunday, 10 am to 1 pm and 2:30 to 6:30 pm).

Two smaller glass-works are the **Verrerie du Vieux Moulin** (93.33.79.51), and the **Verrerie Luzoro** (93.33.79.51), both closed at lunchtime.

You can spend a nice hour or two in the village of Biot itself, so take the time to walk up to the central square, and have a drink or a meal under the arcades.

Just outside Biot, the **Musée Fernand Léger**, entirely devoted to Léger's work, will delight the fans of this painter of tubular masterpieces (Open 10 to 12 and 2.30 to 6.30 pm; closed on Tuesdays).

THE HIPPODROME OF CAGNES-SUR-MER

A race-track just 30 yards from the sea! In summer there are trotters at night, under the spotlights, with the cool sea-breeze coming in across the turf.

MUSEE RENOIR

Les Colettes, the house where Renoir lived in Cagnes for the last fifteen years of his life, on the hill opposite the *Château* , among the olive groves (follow the avenue Auguste Renoir out of the town-centre, then follow the signs to the left up the avenue des Colettes). For art-lovers and sentimentalists.

THE HAUT DE CAGNES AND THE CASTLE

Modern Cagnes is traffic-choked and faceless, and cut in half by the *autoroute*. But if you lift your head over the houses, you'll see the battlements of a fairy castle bedecked with flags. The **Château** dominates the old city, the **Haut de Cagnes**, which is both peaceful and picturesque. Take a walk around in the evening, and reserve a table in one of the many excellent restaurants. See our chapter, **Eating Out**.

The castle itself is often closed (though theoretically only on Tuesdays). It houses an art-gallery and an unusual **Musée de l'Olive** (everything to do with growing and pressing olives), and, in summer, an **international painting exhibition** which is always full of exuberant and unusual works of art. A lot of fun.

THE WALLS OF SAINT PAUL

If you intend to visit only one hilltop village on the French Riviera, there is a good chance you have already chosen Saint Paul. If you are coming in summer or at the weekend, our advice is to try and avoid the crowds. Come early in the morning (before 10), between one and two pm, or at sunset. Stay off the central street (**rue Grande**), and walk around by the church, or on the edge of the village. Saint Paul is built in the shape of a boat, and is completely surrounded by impressive ramparts. In fact, it's possible to walk all the way around on the top of these walls. You will see signs telling you that you do so at your own risk, but only the infirm and the drunk need seriously fear for their safety. From these walls you get a fastastic view of the countryside around, and also of the houses and gardens of the village.

THE MAEGHT FOUNDATION

After you have figured out how to pronounce it (most French people will understand if you say, "mugged"), and how to find it (it's not actually in Saint Paul, but a little down the road, hidden by the trees), you still need several hours to visit this very Mediterranean museum, with its open patios under the shade of the pines. By far the best museum of 20th-century art on the Riviera. (Open 10 am to 12:30 pm and 3 to 7 pm).

THE MATISSE CHAPEL

La Chapelle de la Rosaire is just outside Vence on the road towards Saint Jeannet. It's not a museum, but a real chapel run by nuns, so if you're Catholic, the best day to visit is on Sunday (10 o'clock mass). It is very bare and simple, and has stained-glass windows by Matisse. The effect is difficult to describe. (Open to the public Tuesdays and Thursdays 10 to 11:30 am and 2:30 to 5:30 pm).

While you're in Vence, go shopping for local items of food in the old town. **Rue du Marché** is so narrow in places that you can reach out with your hands and pick fruit out of the shops on each side. You may well be tempted to.

THE BAOU OF SAINT JEANNET

The *Baou* is the big rock that looks like it's going to fall onto the village. To get to the top, you can take the mule-track that winds up the little valley (about 50 minutes to get to the top), or else put on your climbing-boots and go straight up. Either way, the view from the top is worth it.

THE BEACHES AND THE SEA

GOLFE JUAN

At the Cannes end of the sea-front, there are a few hundred yards of sandy, public beach. In July and August, this stretch is rather less crowded than Juan-les-Pins, though there are plenty of people all the same! Golfe Juan is not an exciting resort, but a pleasant place to be when the sun shines, with a number of average-to-good restaurants (including **Chez Nounou** and **La Vache Enragée**), serving sea-food specialties on the sea-front and under the plane trees.

JUAN-LES-PINS

Juan-les-Pins wakes up from its winter hibernation in April, goes into high gear in June, and doesn't decelerate till mid September. Strictly for crowd-lovers and for the young at heart. The sand of the main public beach cannot be seen for bodies, but there's more room to breathe on the private beaches.

All private beaches serve drinks and snacks, at the bar or on your mattress under a parasol. Beaches are relaxed and friendly places to while away an afternoon, and it doesn't really matter which one you choose. The **Ruban Bleu** is one of the bigger ones, with a restaurant, and tables set out on the Promenade. The **Juanita** has pedal-boats, video-games and ping-pong. The **Neptune** has a jetty for sunbathing, water-skiing and a terrifying sport where you are hauled into the air on a parachute. The **Bijou** is a quieter beach, a little out of Juan on the Bord de Mer towards Golfe Juan, and also has a restaurant.

Average prices: Mattress – 32 F/ full day; 24 F/half. Parasol – 14 F/full day; 8 F/half. Pedal-boat – 40 F/hour; 25 F/ half-hour.

From Juan-les-Pins, you can also take a boat to the **Iles de Lérins** (see chapter on **Cannes**).

CAP D'ANTIBES

There are little beaches off the road at various points around the Cap. With a little perseverance, swimmers and lovers of privacy can find rocky coves where they are virtually alone. A good place to start from is the **Beach Plage**, just below the *Musée Naval*. This is not really a beach, but a concrete dock for swimmers and windsurfers to launch off from. It has a nice little snack/restaurant serving salads, and a magnificent view of the Bay of Juan.

If the wind is blowing the wrong way, cross the Cap to the private beaches on the **Plage de la Garoupe**, more classy and much more peaceful than the beaches of Juan-les-Pins. An added advantage for poor swimmers or parents is that the water gets deep very gradually. The biggest beach is the **Plage Keller**, a big beach with a terrace that's covered or open depending on the weather, and a wooden platform for sunbathers who don't like sand. The restaurant is open as early as April, and has a menu at 90 F including fresh fish.

Closer to Antibes, there is the **Plage de la Salis** and the **Plage de l'Ilette**. The latter used to be rather bleak and bare, but is undergoing a face-lift at the time of writing.

ANTIBES TO VILLENEUVE-LOUBET

As you drive from Antibes towards Nice along the sea-road, you have a long (over 6 kilometers) stretch of pebbled beach on your right. The number of beach-goers is limited by the number of cars that can park along the side of the road, so it's a place you can set out your rubber mattresses, your surfboard and your picnic table without bothering anyone else. Bring everything you need, because there's not a shop in sight.

CROS-DE-CAGNES AND SAINT LAURENT DU VAR

More pebbles at Cros-de-Cagnes, which is not a fashionable resort, but has some nice sea-food restaurants (notably **Charlot 1er**). Saint Laurent has been developed in the last few years. The beach is a favorite place for windsurfers, and, for this reason, definitely not recommended for swimmers.

HANGING AROUND THE HEART OF THE RIVIERA: CAFES, BARS AND OTHER PLACES TO SPEND TIME DOING NOTHING SPECIAL

Cafés are better than the cinema. For four or five francs, the price of a coffee, you can have a front-row view of human life, an infinite number of plots running simultaneously before your very eyes. You can see scenes of childhood, the passion of young love, hilarious marital comedy, and drama worthy of the greatest latin films. The backdrops and costumes are Hollywood, Renoir or Fellini, depending on your mood.

Wherever you go, be sure to plan time for just sitting and watching. If you really want to get into the mood, learn to drink *pastis*, the aniseed drink lightened with iced water that goes down so easily on summer afternoons. If you still want to be on your feet by dinner-time, stick to beer or orange-juice.

PLACE NATIONALE, ANTIBES

Our first recommendation is a place you would go to eat rather than to drink. In summer, the restaurants of the Place Nationale in the old town peacefully invade this quiet, shady square with their tables. No haute cuisine, but good simple food served with a smile, at the **Tire-Bouchon** and the **Caméo**. Around 2:30 in the afternoon, as you sip your coffee or liqueurs, and lean back to watch the light breeze blow in the trees, it's a good time to count *les plaisirs de la vie*.

CENTRAL JUAN-LES-PINS

During the day, you can watch the beachwear fashion-show and the parade of the bronzed and beautiful from any sidewalk café (such as the **Neptunia** or the **Tropic** on the *Bord de Mer*, or the **Terrasse de la Jetée** on the *Promenade du Soleil*.

After 10 pm, head for the **Pam Pam** (see **Nightlife**).

MARINA BAIE DES ANGES

The striking architecture of the pyramid-shaped marina at Villeneuve-Loubet cannot fail to attract your attention, favourably or otherwise. Once inside, it is less intimidating and you can go and admire the boats or pick out your choice of apartment from a quayside café.

PORT SAINT LAURENT

The new port of Saint Laurent has taken off in a big way, and is beginning to rival Juan-les-Pins as a place to hang around. Much less "beachy" and more "boaty", though. It's too soon to give the best addresses, so drift around and choose what you like the look of.

PLACE DU CHATEAU, HAUT DE CAGNES

Nice view. Nice cafés. Nice to sit down after traipsing around the castle. The most comfortable chairs are in **Jimmy's**, and the most interesting atmosphere in **Le Bistrot du Guinchoir**

CAFE DE LA PLACE, SAINT PAUL-DE-VENCE

A real old-fashioned café, with marble tables, and old-style French waiters in black coats and white aprons. The terrace gives onto the *terrain de boules* , where the locals play and argue as if there were no tourists at all. Among the locals, you may well spot residents Donald Pleasance or Yves Montand. The café terrace is also a haunt for other stars of the screen, and for the big names of the artistic world.

PLACE CLEMENCEAU, VENCE

You can't get here by car, so park as close to the old city as you can, and walk. You can sit out in the sun or under the trees and admire the houses around the square, the *Mairie* and the old cathdral. If you're feeling strong, there are also some nice things to see inside the cathedral. Then wander down **rue du Marché**, with its picturesque food-shops, and have another drink under the trees in the **Place du Grand Jardin**.

PLACE DE LA LIBERATION, TOURETTES

Take a walk around the village, and get chatting with the local artists and artisans. Offer to discuss your purchase over a drink, and they'll probably take you to the **Café du Midi.** The **Café Cresp** next door is nice too, but for some reason less favoured by the artistic community.

SOMETHING TO TAKE HOME

In these small towns and villages, there is no big-time shopping (the biggest centre is the shopping mall of Cap 3000 not far from Nice Airport), and the locals usually go into Nice or Cannes to buy clothes or stylish articles.

If you keep your eyes open, though, you can find interesting things to buy as presents, or as decoration for the home. The villages are full of little craftsmen, sometimes working in the shops that sell their wares. Have a look around the markets too. As well as interesting food, there are stalls selling new and used clothes, belts, bags, jewelry, lace, linen, and assorted gadgets — a lot of junk, and a lot of really nice things too.

Go to Juan-les-Pins for beachware and casual summer clothes; to Vallauris for pottery; to Biot for glass; to Saint Paul for decorative jewelry; to Tourettes for printed fabrics. The list below, starting at Juan and moving northwards, is a selection to whet your appetite.

SHOPPING BY THE SEA, JUAN-LES-PINS

On boulevard Guillaumont, beach fashions at **Arianie**, and clothes made-on-the-Riviera at **Chacok** and **Fleur de Rhum**. The avenue Guy de Maupassant is for the young and trendy, with shops like **Zoo**, **Chipie**, **Pink Fly** and **Cactus**.

FOR YOUNG CHILDREN, ANTIBES

In rue James Close (a pedestrian street) there are a couple of very nice little toy-shops, including **Pierrot-la-Lune**, with toys from central Europe and Scandinavia.

The **Armoire à Linge** at 6, boulevard Wilson has beautiful clothes for children, and the **Bibus** store at n° 13 also has a good selection.

BRIC-A-BRAC

The word in French is *brocante*, and you'll find these shops all over, selling a mixture of valueless junk and priceless antiques. The most original is probably **Le Roy Soleil**, on the RN7 betwen Antibes and the Biot railway-station (460, avenue de Nice. Tel: 93.33.45.41). You can't miss it: the pavement outside is adorned with prancing horses, Corinthian columns and a huge globe of the earth. Owner Jean de Roumilly is 74 years old and started up his curious establishment with the encouragement of Jean Cocteau and Florence Gould. While it's difficult to buy anything there (asking the price of things is not really done), one can well understand that the Victorine Film Studios in Nice have made good use of his place over the last 35 years. Several other *brocantes* have opened in the vicinity, but none has quite the same style.

La Colle-sur-Loup is also famous for brocante and antiques. Park anywhere near the centre and walk around. The village is not nearly as picturesque as nearby Saint Paul, but there is a much higher chance of your finding a bargain.

ARTS & CRAFTS, SAINT PAUL

Saint Paul has attracted all kinds of crafts shops, ranging from the wonderful to the very tasteless. Three of the nicer shops in rue Grande are: **Les Petites Maisons de Provence**, which sells scale models of Provençal village houses that can be put together to make up a village. All are hand-made, and no two houses are exactly alike; **Le Puits**, selling unusual ceramic cats and creatures; and, **Bulles**, selling very fine handmade jewelry.

La Rose des Vents, offering an enchanting collection of straw hats, boaters, Panamas, dainty veiled creations, flowery bonnets and many more models. All shapes and sizes, in a shop that is a little too crowded for comfort.

Then there are the galleries. If you are serious about art, have a browse around, then stop *chez* **Catherine Issert** (at the entrance to the village), recognized as the best spotter of new and rising local talent. Other serious gallery-owners are **Frédéric Gollong**, in rue Grande, and **Alexandre de la Salle** not far from the Maeght Foundation.

FOOD AND PRESERVES, VENCE

Vence is something of a local gastronomic centre, and delicatessens like **La Taste** (9, avenue de la Résistance) sell a variety of goodies in jars and bottles, made according to local recipes.

THE ARTISANS OF TOURETTES

Unlike many of the things you see in Saint Paul, everything here is made on the spot: in pottery, fabric, leather, pewter or copper. Among the weavers who work in the shops where they sell: **Hélène Chenard** who makes beautifully coloured clothes, scarves, shawls and even ties (10, Grande rue); **Frédérique de**

Cayeux, who will make you a wool jacket for about 1500 F, and a jacket and skirt in cotton for about 1300 F (1, Impasse de la Grande Rue). **Cha Tsaou** who can weave you a wall-hanging or a bedspread (18, Grande rue).

Perhaps the most famous artisans of Tourettes, however, are **HélènePaillard** and **Jeanine David** (2, rue des Coustasses) who make cushions which are quite expensive, but worth a special trip just to see.

INFORMATION, SPECIAL EVENTS

For more information about any of the towns or villages mentioned above, get in touch with the local tourist offices (*Syndicats d'Initiative*) who can provide you with detailed maps, brochures in English, and information about the local events taking place.

SYNDICATS D'INITIATIVE

Antibes: 93.33.95.64
Juan-les-Pins: 93.67.04.98
Golfe Juan: 93.63.73.12
Vallauris: 93.63.82.58
Valbonne: 93.42.00.19
Cagnes-sur-Mer: 93.20.67.64
Vence: 93.58.69.30

David Ward-Perkins

DAVID WARD-PERKINS is a freelance writer and journalist working on the French Riviera. His special fields are high-tech business, education and tourism.

"It's so beautiful only one word comes to mind at a time like this: dough..."

5
THE FESTIVAL CITY: CANNES AND THE CANNOIS REGION

104	Where to Stay
107	Interesting Things To Do in Cannes
109	The Beaches and the Sea
110	Hanging Around in Cannes
111	Excursions: The Lérins Islands
	Mougins
	Grasse
	Gorges du Loup
114	Something to Take Home

Cannes is the Beverly Hills of the French Riviera, with the same luxurious atmosphere and the same entertainment industry glamour. But that's not all — Cannes also has the blue, blue Mediterranean (who says it's polluted?) and French cuisine, including one of the finest restaurants in the region.

People come to Cannes for the beautiful sandy beaches, rare on a coast that in most places has a pebbly shoreline. People come for **La Croisette**, the palm-tree-lined seaside promenade that is the center of all activity. They come for any of the series of national and international congresses, conferences and festivals that take place in the **Palais des Festivals**, the large pink concrete edifice, known unaffectionately to old timers as *the bunker*, at the west end of the *Croisette*.

The biggest of the year-long round of professional gatherings in Cannes is the world's largest film festival, in May. Second in importance is the **MIDEM** (International Market for Records and Music Publishers) in January, followed by **MIPTV** (International Market for TV Programs) in April and **MIPCOM** (International Market for TV, Cable and Satellite Programs) in October. During these events, Cannes is full of people, not just the participants, both famous and unknown, but also residents and visitors to the *Côte d'Azur*, who come to Cannes to be where the action is.

WHERE TO STAY

The most fashionable place to stay in Cannes is at one of the palace hotels on the *Croisette*. You're right in the center of the action with, if you're willing to pay a bit extra, a very fine view of the sea. The terraces in front of these hotels are the best places from which to watch the passing parade. They have gardens, swimming pools, private beaches with restaurants, and night clubs, as well as the hairdressers and boutiques that are standard in luxury hotels. And the best restaurants in Cannes are in two of the *grands palaces*: **Le Royal Gray** (two stars) at the **Gray d'Albion** and **La Palme d'Or** (one star) at the Martinez.

If you'd like a quieter, less grand place to stay in Cannes, there are some pleasant smaller hotels, centrally located but off the *Croisette* . The small hotels listed here do not have restaurants and the rooms are small, but the staffs are friendly. These are the places where many local expatriates put up their guests.

HIGH-LIFE ON THE CROISETTE

HOTEL CARLTON

58, La Croisette
Tel: 93.68.91.68

This elegant *grande dame* of the palaces was recently bought by Inter-Continental, which is putting a lot of money into restoring it. 335 rooms from 750 F for a single facing the mountains to 1570 F for a double on the seafront. Also facing the sea, *grand luxe* suites with sitting rooms from 3,225 F to 5,390 F. Lower rates in winter. Restaurant **La Côte** has an attractive circular dining room, an elegant terrace and good traditional cuisine.

LE MAJESTIC

6, La Croisette
Tel: 93.68.91.00

Perhaps the most popular of the beautifully restored *grands hôtels* on the *Croisette*. Across from the new *Palais des Festivals*. Heated seawater pool and garden, private beach facing the Iles de Lérins. 262 air-conditioned rooms from 1,000 F to 1,600 F. 12 suites.

HOTEL MARTINEZ

73, La Croisette

Tel: 93.68.91.91

One of the palace hotels, recently restored in Art Deco style. 400 rooms from 700 F to 2,000 F. 15 suites from 3,000 F to 8,000 F. Rates lower in winter. Restaurant **La Palme d'Or** is one of best in Cannes. **L'Orangeraie** serves pool-side lunches and dinners. Private beach restaurant serves buffet lunch.

LE GRAY d'ALBION

38, rue des Serbes

Tel: 93.68.54.54

Cannes' newest luxury hotel is set back from the sea front, behind the *de luxe* shopping mall, **Les Boutiques de Gray Street**, which opens onto the *Croisette.* 187 rooms 1,200 to 1,400 F. 14 suites. **Le Royal Gray** is the best restaurant in Cannes, **Les 4 Saisons** serves French and Lebanese dishes, **Le Jane's** is a popular nightclub that also serves dinner.

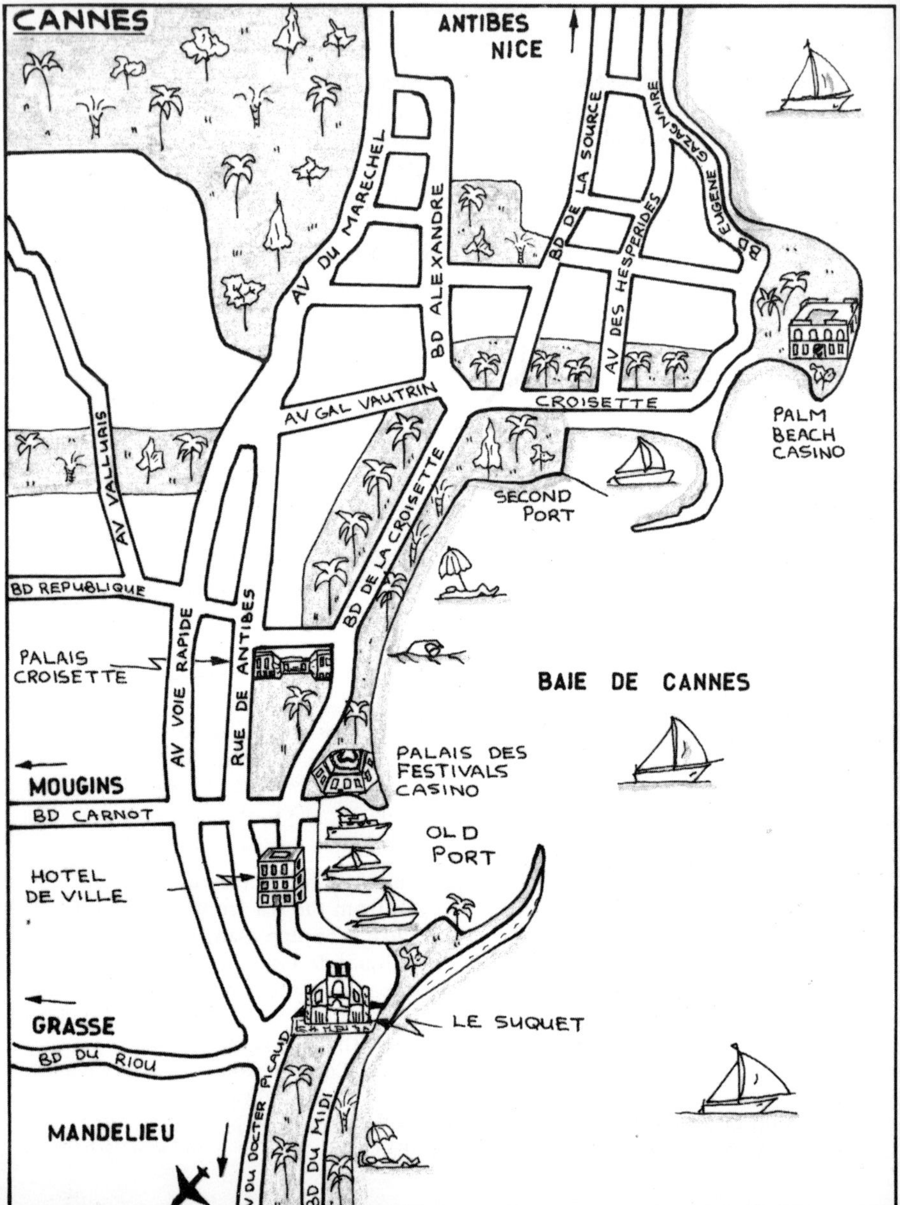

CANNES
ANTIBES
NICE
AV DU MARECHEL
BD ALEXANDRE
BD DE LA SOURCE
BD EUGENE GAZAGNAIRE
AV DES HESPERIDES
AV GAL VAUTRIN
CROISETTE
PALM
BEACH
CASINO
AV VALLURIS
SECOND
PORT
BD DE LA CROISETTE
BD REPUBLIQUE
PALAIS
CROISETTE
AV VOIE RAPIDE
RUE DE ANTIBES
BAIE DE CANNES
PALAIS DES
FESTIVALS
CASINO
MOUGINS
BD CARNOT
OLD
PORT
HOTEL
DE VILLE
GRASSE
LE SUQUET
BD DU RIOU
AV DU DOCTER PICAUD
BD DU MIDI
MANDELIEU

BEING MORE REASONABLE

HOTEL VICTORIA
122, rue d'Antibes
Tel: 93.99.36.36

25 air-conditioned rooms from 335 F to 545 F. Small pool and pleasant American bar. No restaurant.

LE CANBERRA
120, rue d'Antibes
Tel: 93.38.20.70/72

44 air-conditioned rooms from 260 F to 465 F. Under same management as the **Victoria**, whose pool is available to guests here. No restaurant.

LE MOLIERE
5-7, rue Molière
Tel: 93.38.16

This small hotel has 34 rooms with terraces and a pleasant garden. Rooms from 205 F to 350 F. No restaurant.

HOTEL DE PROVENCE
9, rue Molière
Tel: 93.38.44.35

Near the old *Palais des Festivals*, this small hotel is decorated in *Provençal* style and has modern comforts of TV and minibar in each room. Garden. Bar and restaurant. 30 rooms from 170 F to 330 F.

LE VENDOME
37, boulevard d'Alsace
Tel: 93.38.34.33

Pleasant small hotel, away from the *Croisette,* off the boulevard de la République. 14 rooms from 190 F to 500 F.

LE MAS CANDILLE
Boulevard Rebuffel
06250 Mougins
Tel: 93.90.00.85

For a real retreat, try this *Provençal* farmhouse on a hill 15 minutes by car from Cannes. Surrounded by beautiful trees and flowers, with pool, terraces and a good restaurant featuring regional specialties, the inn has 24 unpretentious rooms. 500 F for a double room with bath, 700-820 F for a suite with terrace.

INTERESTING THINGS TO DO IN CANNES

It's worth straying from the *Croisette* long enough to walk along the **Old Port**. You can admire the boats and perhaps shop in some

of the ship's chandlers for striped Breton jerseys and other nautical clothing or handsome brass fixtures. One of the best fish restaurants in Cannes is **Pierrot 1er**, at 53, rue Félix-Faure, behind the Port. Also in this area is the **Marché Forville**, Cannes' colorful open-air market (only open in the mornings). Apart from fruit and vegetables, you can also find cheap clothes and amusing bric-à-brac.

Just west of the Port is **Le Suquet**, the picturesque old town of Cannes. The narrow streets winding their way up Mont Chevalier are lined with restaurants and shops. From the rue Perissol one has a good view of the port and at the top is the **Musée de la Castre**, an anthropological museum with Mediterranean and Latin American collections.

THE BEACHES AND THE SEA

On the beaches, even women in the briefest of bathing suits wear their jewels, perhaps turquoise or shell necklaces bought from beach vendors or gold leather sandals. The clean sand beaches are dotted with umbrellas and mattresses in a rainbow of colors — now yellow or pink, now blue and white striped — marking the limits of the series of private beaches along the *Croisette*. There are also free public beaches at the west end of the *Croisette*, some quieter ones around the headland of **Le Suquet**, and rocky coves on towards **Cap d'Antibes**.

ONDINE-PLAGE
15, La Croisette
Tel: 93.94.23.15 and 93.94.00.49
Lunch only

This, the best of the beach restaurants, is popular even on gray days. Beautiful beach with yellow parasols and chic sunbathers.

PLAGE SPORTIVE
La Croisette
Tel: 93.38.63.73

Lively beach with blue and white parasols, near the old *Palais des Festivals* . Cold buffet is a good buy.

PLAGE CLUB DES SPORTS
La Croisette
Tel: 93.38.59.72

Red and white colors on this rather sporty beach, equipped for volley ball and ping pong, in the center of the *Croisette*. Snack lunches are rather high priced.

LE VOILIER
La Croisette
Tel: 93.94.25.46

Well maintained beach by the Carlton's, with blue and white colors. Preppy clientele (called in French *BCBG: Bon Chic, Bon Genre*). High-priced lunches.

PLAGE DU MARTINEZ
La Croisette
Tel: 93.68.91.91

Beach with the most services: water skiing, parachuting, massage, boat rides. Hot buffet lunch.

CANNES-BEACH
La Croisette
Tel: 93.38.14.59

Most popular beach on the *Croisette*. Green and white decor, regional cuisine, reasonable prices. *Aïoli*, raw vegetables to dip in garlic mayonnaise, is an excellent choice.

PLAGE DU GRAY d'ALBION
La Croisette
Tel: 93.99.15.15

Jacques Chibois, of the hotel's two-star restaurant, also supervises the menu at the beach restaurant.

HANGING AROUND IN CANNES

Cannes is all on the surface: what you see is what you get. And what you see looks bright and sparkling and expensive. There are pink and white storybook palace hotels for real princesses (Arab) and moguls (Hollywood), fronted by terraces on which royalty and commoners alike spend hours bronzing in the sun.

Even when not on the beaches, people are outside all the time, strolling under the palms by the seaside, shopping along the landward side, or sitting in one of the terrace cafés or restaurants that line the *Croisette* (especially the **Blue Bar** or the **Festival**). The terraces of the palace hotels are always good spots for seeing and being seen.

EXCURSIONS

If all the glitter and glamour of Cannes become too much, there are two easy escape routes to calmer areas of the *région cannoise*:

across the sea to the **Iles de Lérins** or up into the hills of the back country.

The Lerins Islands

The **Iles de Lérins** are only a kilometer away, but the green quiet of the eucalyptus and pine groves and the clear waters of the nearly deserted beaches make you think you're a world away from the crowds on the *Croisette.* Boats leave from the Port (Compagnie Esterel Chanteclair, Tel: 93.39.11.82) about ten times a day, beginning at 7:00 am and return to Cannes hourly in the afternoon, with the last boat leaving at 7:00 pm. The round trip is 20 F to the big island, **Sainte Marguerite**, and 25 F if you include a visit to the smaller **Saint Honorat**. The short boat ride, about 15 minutes to Sainte Marguerite, is spectacular, with a view of Cannes and the whole coastline from Cap Roux to the Cap d'Antibes.

Sainte Marguerite has several nice walks to points of interest, including the five-mile complete tour of the island. The fortress, which once imprisoned the Man in the Iron Mask, is worth a visit. There are lovely beaches for picnics and swimming, particularly at the far end, away from the docks.

Saint Honorat is interesting principally for its monastery. The island is named for Saint Honorat, who sought refuge there in the fourth century and established a monastery when he was joined by others. The present Cistercian monastery has, since the late nineteenth century, surrounded the ruins of the ancient ones. The monks in their black and white habits live the same life and say the same prayers as the disciples of Saint Honorat. The monastery museum and several of its ancient chapels can be visited.

Mougins

Just 7 kilometers North of Cannes is **Mougins**, a medieval hilltop village that has become a gastronomic center since Roger Vergé opened his **Moulin de Mougins** nearly 20 years ago. One of the best restaurants in France, the three-star Moulin has attracted other chefs and now gourmets and gourmands have a choice of eating well in either of two mill houses, a stage stop, or a farm, at prices ranging from around 300 F to twice that. The drive to Mougins is short enough to put it within range for dinner, but you may find it easier to get reservations for lunch. Eating on the sunny flowery terraces of any of these restaurants, preceded or followed by a stroll through the little village, is a lovely way to spend part of a day.

Located in a sixteenth-century olive mill set down off the D3 from Cannes to Mougins, there is the two-star **L'Amandier de Mougins** in the old village, whose terrace has a magnificent view over the valley to the *Alpes Maritimes*. There is also the **Relais de Mougins**, a very attractive one-star restaurant on the Place de la Mairie in the village, and the **Ferme de Mougins**, below the village in a garden setting. See the **Eating Out** chapter for restaurant details.

The two Boutiques de Roger Vergé, at the **Moulin** and in the village, sell food products such as special spices and conserves, as well as Vergé's cookbook (in English).

Grasse

Another pleasant day-trip from Cannes is up to **Grasse** (17 kilometers from Cannes) and beyond. Grasse is where the basic floral essences of the French perfume industry are concocted from flowers, plants, and animal products of the region and of the whole world. The small town (pop. 38,000) is terraced down the hillside and has spectacular views all the way to the sea. A visit in the morning will permit you to catch the daily (except Sundays) flower market on the **Place aux Aires** in the old part of town. Colorful umbrellas shelter many of the flower-filled stands that run down both sides of the Place. A cup of coffee at one of the cafés beside the fountain makes a nice pause, before shopping for picnic supplies, perhaps *comté* and other cheeses from **La**

Fromagerie (5, rue de l'Oratoire), and heading up the **Gorges du Loup** for a picnic.

A visit, at no charge, to one of the perfume factories (**Fragonard**, **Molinard**) may be of interest, although the tour guide rushes the groups through the factory to the gift shop. There you can buy perfumes, colognes, pure flower essences, soaps, bath salts, etc. The scents are also sold in the metal containers used for long-term storage, which are nice for travel.

Gorges du Loup

Stop for your picnic somewhere in the vicinity of **Gourdon** (9 miles above Grasse via the D3), a tiny village perched on a rocky spur jutting out into the **Gorges du Loup**. The village has been tastefully restored and contains little shops selling herbs, soaps, olive oil, and some quite good jams like *clémentine* (tangerine), *griottes* (sour cherry), *pamplemousse* (grapefruit)... The real attraction of Gourdon, however, is its little jewel of a *château* (open 2 pm to 6 pm, guided tour in English, 10 F entrance).

Construction of the unusal trapezoidal fortress began in the ninth century and continued in waves through the next 700 years. In 1918 it was bought by May Norris, a wealthy American, who began the work of restoration at the same time that Henry and Mary Clews were restoring the *château* at La Napoule, which had also belonged to the Villeneuve family. The small rooms of this miniature castle are tastefully furnished with antiques and works of art, including a wood polychrome statue of Saint Sebastian by El Greco, strangely elongate (some believe it is because the artist was astigmatic or maybe the statue was intended to be seen from below). From its formal gardens, one has a dramatic view of green hills and valleys stretching to the sea.

After tea on one of the terrace cafés of Gourdon, you might continue on up the scenic gorge for 15 kilometers to the village of **Gréolières**, which has another spectacular view. As you enter the village by the single street, you can't miss the colorful sign sticking out on the left: **Dick le Tisserand**. A *tisserand* is a weaver and this one is Dutch and speaks English. The intensely colored rugs, wallhangings and table linens are woven by Dick on his loom from his studio with a view down the valley. There are also skirts, jackets, ponchos and sometimes children's clothing made by Dick's wife out of his fabric.

SOMETHING TO TAKE HOME

Cannes is not the place to shop for bargains. Most of the shopping is along the **Croisette** between the Carlton and the Palais des Festivals or in the **rue d'Antibes**, behind and parallel to the Croisette. That's where you'll find the big-name boutiques found in most international capitals and resort areas. The street that has the most avant-garde fashions is the **rue du Commandant André**, between the rue d'Antibes and the Croisette. Emmanuelle Khanh, Giorgio Armani, Céline, Christofle, and Descamps are in the rue d'Antibes. Gucci, Hermès, Christian Dior, Pierre Cardin, and Stéphane Kelian are found in **Les Boutiques de Gray Street**, a *de luxe* shopping mall that goes from the Croisette through to the rue d'Antibes.

There are also some shops exclusive to Cannes or to the region, both in the main shopping streets and scattered nearby. The following is a selected list of some of the most interesting. The pedestrian zone, known as the **rue Meynadier**, has some good food-shops and cheap clothes.

GOLF PLUS

131, rue d'Antibes

A small green shop with a full line of golf equipment and clothing for men and women. The golf bags come in a rainbow of pastel and bright colors.

LA DRAGONNE

131, rue d'Antibes
Tel: 93.38.72.14

Next door to Golf Plus. An antique shop specializing in beautiful swords and other weapons, tin soldiers, medals, Napoleonic prints.

COMPTOIR SUD PACIFIC

121, rue d'Antibes

Toiletries for travelers. Bath products and perfumes, handsome leather kits and cases, Island-print robes, logo beach towels.

SPORTLINE

Rue d'Antibes, corner of
rue Emmanuel Signoret

Ellesse, Fila, Tacchini and other European athletic wear and shoes that tend to be less expensive here than in the U.S.

HALLES CAPONE

105, rue d'Antibes
Tel: 93.38.63.26

The name of this shop can help you remember how to pronounce the French for market: it rhymes with the gangster's name. Trendy unisex fashions. Not inexpensive (1,120 F for an unstructured woven cotton jacket).

REVERIE

79, rue d'Antibes
Tel: 93.39.60.19

Bath accessories, robes, towels. Also bath salts and soaps that make nice portable, unbreakable gifts.

ESPACE CONTEMPORAIN

154, rue d'Antibes
Tel: 93.94.50.76

This attractive boutique of contemporary furniture and furnishings has some good gift ideas.

LA SQUADRA

Les Boutiques de Gray Street

Designed by sisters in Monaco, the clothes sold in these two boutiques (men, women) are bright cottons and knits, very *Côte d'Azur.*

CLAUDE BONUCCI

Les Boutiques de Gray Street
Tel: 93.38.68.28

Bonucci, a native of Nice, has three shops on the *Côte* (Cannes, Nice, Saint-Tropez) where he sells his line of fine men's clothing. Shoes in glovesoft leather, silk and linen jackets and suits, soft lambskin jackets, woven cotton and silk shirts, elegant and unusual formalwear. The smaller line of women's clothes includes delicate suedes and leathers in lovely colors and paillette evening dresses. High quality priced accordingly.

SOULEIADO

Les Boutiques de Gray Street
Tel: 93.99.22.26

Traditional *Provençal* print fabrics that can be bought by the meter or already made up into peasant scarves, skirts, dresses, tablecloths, napkins, placemats, cushions, and accessories. **Souleiado** was founded nearly 50 years ago and its name means "a ray of sunshine piercing the clouds." Now more than 2,000 sales outlets throughout the world.

FLEUR DE RHUM

Les Boutiques de Gray Street

Line of women's clothes by Côte d'Azur designer Arlette Chacok. Bright cottons and knits.

SACHA
Les Boutiques de Gray Street

Women's shoes, mostly by Charles Kammer, including multicolored leather summer flats. Some colorful leather clothing.

CHACOK
7, rue du Commandant André
Tel: 93.68.10.33

Côte d'Azur style in women's clothes: bright colors, exciting prints, simple lines.

LES ARTISANS DU TEMPS PRESENT
35, rue Hoche
Tel: 93.38.23.62

Cotton, silk women's clothing with simple lines.

TEMPORA
7, rue Victor Cousin
Tel: 93.99.06.00

This boutique near the old *Palais des Festivals* has original women's clothing and very helpful sales staff.

CHANTAL THOMASS
32, rue du Commandant André
Tel: 93.99.39.70

Designer very popular with trendy young Parisian women. Cottons and knits in bright colors and sophisticated grays and blacks, silk and lace.

YOHJI YAMAMOTO
116, rue d'Antibes
Tel: 93.38.62.79

Famous Japanese designer's clothes – quite expensive.

FRUIT DE LA PASSION
Les Boutiques de Gray Street

Cacharel and other storybook dresses, to be worn with little straw hats also for sale.

PRUNE
118, rue d'Antibes
Tel: 93.38.63.71

Sweet dresses with white scalloped collars, **Cacharel** rompers, baby sweatsuits.

LES P'TITS DURS
Rue d'Antibes

Next door to **Cacharel**, this shop features wild, trendy clothes for tough little guys and gals.

LA CAPITAINERIE
76, rue Meynadier
Tel: 93.39.27.86

For yacht-owners and all boating enthusiasts, a fine collection of nautical bric-à-brac and gadgets in this newly opened boutique. Also takes orders for *on-board* personalized linen and tableware executed by local artists.

CANNES DUTY FREE
44, La Croisette
Tel: 93.99.59.53

Duty free discounts on a wide assortment of leather goods, jewelry, watches, lighters and pens. Also perfumes, scarves and ties.

LA FERME SAVOYARDE
Fromagerie Ceneri et Fils
22, rue Meynadier
Tel: 93.39.63.68

Famous throughout the whole region, this incredible cheese shop supplies the top restaurants from its stock of something like 300 different cheeses including *chèvre* (goat cheese) – of course. In the afternoons, you can visit the cellars below the shop where the cheeses are matured. Pungent!

AUX BONS RAVIOLIS
31, rue Meynadier
Tel: 93.39.36.63

Fresh pasta made on the premises in all shapes and sizes. Also appetizing take-out dishes. Sheer temptation!

Joanne McNabb

JOANNE MCNABB is a free-lance writer specializing in cultural affairs who lives in St. Paul de Vence.

ANTIQUITES
Choses
Choses
SYNDIC
D'INIT

6
SAINT-TROPEZ: THE STARS AND THE SEA

120	The Port: On or Off Season
122	Who's Who — What's When
123	Where to Stay: Hotels In Town and Out
126	Interesting Things to Do
127	The Beaches and the Sea
162	Cafés and Hang-Outs
164	Something to Take Home
165	Excursions Around Saint-Tropez
167	Haute Provence and the Wine Country

Saint-Tropez, the elegant, the fashionable, is the fishing-village with a difference. The most Parisian of Riviera towns, Saint-Tropez sets trends today that Paris will hear of tomorrow. Saint-Tropez nightlife draws the tycoons from their offices, the idle from their poolside deck-chairs, and the jetset from their jets. Not to mention famous faces and names from three decades of cinematic history.

Quiet in the winter, Saint-Tropez is pleasantly bucolic in spring and autumn, on a road that leads nowhere else, bordered by the hills and vines of the Riviera wine-country — *les Côtes de Provence* . But as May turns to June, the pace picks up, the shops and restaurants close later and later, till Saint-Tropez is one continuous party, spreading across the port and through the town.

The Port – On or Off Season

From mid-July to the end of August the most picturesque, the most painted port of the whole Riviera can barely be seen for visitors. Bumper to bumper, car to coach to caravan, they keep coming, leaving the vehicles in the huge parking lot by the new basin and continuing on foot to gape at pleasure craft lined up by the mega yachts. On board, screened only by monster bouquets of stiff carnations and gladioli, servants in white gloves pour the champagnes, and the yacht-owners and their gorgeous friends ignore the stares.

Between the sidewalk-artists hawking their daubs and the bronze statue of Admiral Suffren glaring out to sea, flows a motley crowd of androgynous models with maxi-dogs and mini-scooters, jaunty retirees in naval caps, green-haired punks and such. If someone goes by with leashes full of dogs and a friend in tow, heads spin. Was that Bardot?

Meanwhile, the quayside boutiques lure vacationers with T-shirts, tricks and baubles, flaunting designs that were all the rage this morning. Will they still be fashionable by this afternoon?

To escape the noise and the shimmering heat, passers-by

succomb under the cool red awnings of the **Café Sénéquier** for their famous *tarte tropézienne*, hunger over the fish list at **l'Escale**, or endure a bit longer to collapse at the small tables of the *crêperies* by the old Portalet watch tower.

The long stroll along the **Jean Réveille** jetty reveals more facets: one devoted owner polishes his own brass while, in the next mooring, young officers in starched white Bermuda shorts and knee socks guard a magnate's floating domain. Watching all, old salts warm themselves and pass the time of day on the stone bench called *le Banc des Mensonges.*

They are a reminder that one should really arrive here by sea for Saint-Tropez is above all a maritime place. For centuries, it was a fiercely independent city that drove off Barbary pirates, then a merchant port that lived from fishing and boat building and transporting wine to Marseille and Toulon. Before the tourist traps and nightclubs, there were boatyards and, in the **Annonciade Chapel**, sailmakers cut and sewed lateen sails. Today 50 fishermen still bring in a daily catch, sell it glistening fresh on the quays or the **Place des Herbes**.

From the lighthouse, the view stretches wide across the Gulf of Saint-Tropez backed by the ranges of the **Maures** and the **Esterel**. With luck and clear skies, you can see snow-capped Alps in the distance. From here too, the crowded port falls into place against an irregular backdrop of ocher and pastel houses protected by the massive **Citadel.** Tourists blur into perspective.

Saint-Tropez's situation on a peninsula long protected it from the coastal railway, from the highways and the impressive promenades found in the rest of the Riviera. Dark pinewoods guarantee the privacy of vast estates, small coves can be reached only by sea, gardens and patios hide behind high walls.

In the corners of the old town, in the leafy lanes between the vineyards, in the shade of the harbour wall, the fishing village that first attracted writers and painters lives on. In spite of its long love-affair with stars and stardom, Saint-Tropez retains potent charm and hidden delights.

Who's Who – What's When

SAINT-TROPEZ — a misspelling. Torpes was the real name of the Roman officer and martyr beheaded under nasty Nero. The headless body drifted here by boat in the company of a dog and a rooster as shown by naive sculptures in the church.

BRAVADE I — a local festivity from May 16 to May 18. The polychrome bust of the Saint, complete with military mustache and crown, is aired in grand procession with much drumming and firing of ancient muskets. The ones that explode are layed away in the church for keeps.

BRAVADE II — on June 15 the town celebrates the rout of 22 Spanish galleys by the determined Saint-Tropez militia in 1637. More drums, fifes, parades, fierce musket and cannon volleys.

SUFFREN — Pierre André de Suffren, Knight of Malta, Marquis of Saint-Tropez, was the full name and title of the outspoken, barrel-shaped naval officer who fought in the Mediterranean against Barbary pirates, and in the Caribbean for America's independence, to be finally sent to the Indies to battle the English and become an admiral. His statue was made from 6000 enemy cannons.

MAUPASSANT — writer of short stories with a fine twist was a keen sailor who explored this coast before it became famous and described the *modest* port that smelled of fish and tar in *Sur L'Eau*.

PAUL SIGNAC — an Impressionist with pointillist leanings who also came by sea and found the strong light, colors and reflections of the harbor so irresistible that he settled here and invited his friends **BONNARD, MATISSE, DUFY** and **DUNOYER DE SEGONZAC** whose works now hang in the Museum.

COLETTE — spent summers here in her villa, La Treille Muscate, quietly indulging in and writing about its garden scents and *provençal* flavors.

PAUL POIRET — *couturier* of the twenties, playwright **JEAN**

COCTEAU and society gravitated here between the wars. After World War II, came a new wave, fresh faces of which **FRANCOISE SAGAN, BRIGITTE BARDOT** and **ROGER VADIM** were the most obvious. **AZNAVOUR, EDDIE BARCLAY, CLAUDE BRASSEUR, REGINE** and newer billings like **GRACE JONES** and **ELTON JOHN** with their hangers-on now appear from the world of show business.

NIOULARGUE — An imaginative week of yachting events in mid-September that attracts the maxi-sloops and trimarans. The newest *Saint-Trop* pretext for celebrations to add to a filled summer calendar.

WHERE TO STAY

Our first choice would be a private retreat belonging to a friend, complete with cypresses, olive-groves and swimming-pool. Second choice, the cabin of your own yacht, or a passenger cabin on the **Sea Goddess**. The same quiet exclusiveness and privacy can also be found in some Tropezian hotels, away from the crowds, in the sanctuary of their huge inner patios, or set in landscaped gardens outside the town.

IN TOWN

BYBLOS

Avenue Paul Signac
Tel: 94.97.00.04
Telex 470235
Open: Apr 17 to Nov 2

In the heart of the town, a cluster of whitewashed houses furnished with antiques, this millionaire's village is within a toss of the Place des Lices where the locals let the celebrities join them for a leisurely game of *pétanque*. Central swimming-pool. Lifts. Two restaurants, **Le Chabichou** and **La Braiserie**. 100 rooms and 10 suites. 760-1770 F. Night-club, **Les Caves du Roy** and disco.

LA RESIDENCE LES LICES

Avenue Auguste Grandgeon
Tel: 94.97.28.28
Open: Easter to Oct 15

A central, comfortable choice with swimming-pool. 34 rooms 320-650 F.

YACA

1, boulevard Aumale
Tel: 94.97.11.79
Telex 462140
Open: Apr 15 to Oct 15

Just below the Citadel, this restored

ST TROPEZ

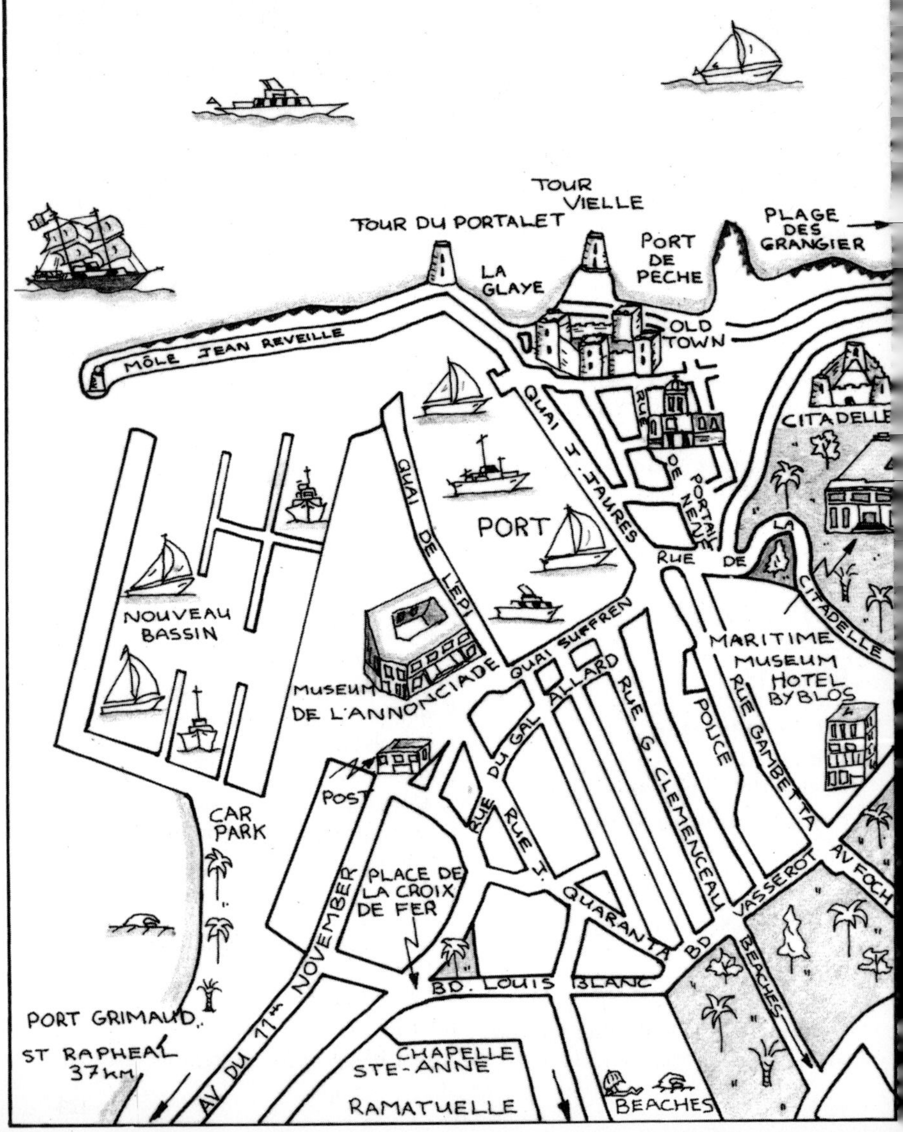
TOUR VIELLE
TOUR DU PORTALET
PLAGE DES GRANGIER
PORT DE PECHE
LA GLAYE
OLD TOWN
MÔLE JEAN REVEILLE
CITADELLE
QUAI J. JAURES
RUE DE PORTAIL NEUF
QUAI DE L'EPI
PORT
LA
RUE DE CITADELLE
NOUVEAU BASSIN
MARITIME MUSEUM
HOTEL BYBLOS
QUAI SUFFREN
MUSEUM DE L'ANNONCIADE
RUE DU GAL ALLARD
RUE G. CLEMENCEAU
POLICE
RUE GAMBETTA
POST
CAR PARK
RUE J. QUARANTA
BD VASSEROT
AV FOCH
PLACE DE LA CROIX DE FER
AV DU 11th NOVEMBER
BD. LOUIS BLANC
BEACHES
PORT GRIMAUD
ST RAPHEAL 37KM
CHAPELLE STE-ANNE
RAMATUELLE
BEACHES

town dwelling has delightfully decorated rooms with balconies that give on an inner court. No restaurant. Pool. 22 rooms from 750-970 F.

LA PONCHE
Place Révelin
Tel: 94.97.02.53
Open: Apr 1 to Oct 15

Facing the animated square by the fishing harbour, this attractively renovated hotel with a terrace where Picasso used to come may be noisy at times, but ideally central and equipped with kitchenettes. Restaurant. 23 rooms from 280-640 F.

AROUND SAINT-TROPEZ

MAS DE CHASTELAS
3.5 km on road to Gassin
Tel: 94.56.09.11
Telex 461516
Open: May to Sept

The XVIIth century building dates back to the time when silk was a local industry. The rooms have been converted and furnished in a light-hearted cottage style. Gardens. Pool. Tennis. Service attentive but unobtrusive. Lunch: 130 F. Dinner: 240 F. 21 rooms 400-1250 F.

RESIDENCE DE LA PINEDE
1 km near La Bouillabaisse Beach
Tel: 94.97.04.21
Telex 470489
Open: Apr 15 to Oct 1

A quiet place with a pool of its own. Restaurant. 40 rooms 500-1300 F. 5 suites.

LE LEVANT
2.5 km along the Route de Salins
Tel: 94.97.33.33
Open: Mar 22 to Oct 12

Lovely gardens with a view and a pool. 28 rooms 320-525 F.

LA TARTANE
3 km along the Route de Salins
Tel: 94.97.21.23
Open: March 15 to Nov 5

With a poolside garden. 12 rooms 395-525 F.

LA MANDARINE
4 km, near Tahiti Beach
Tel: 94.97.21.00
Telex 970461
Open: Easter to Oct 15

A clutch of *provençal* bungalows around a pool and with a view. 40 rooms 720-1400 F. Restaurant: 180/275 F.

LA FERME D'AUGUSTIN
4 km, near Tahiti Beach
Tel: 94.97.18.12

Conveniently close to the super beaches. 35 rooms. 310-500 F.

LE BAOU
12 km near Ramatuelle
Tel: 94.79.20.48

Telex 462152
Closed: mid-Nov to mid-Dec

In a modern décor, its balconies and terraced pool view the sea high above Pampelonne. 36 rooms from 360-850 F.

PONTE ROMANO
19 km
Plan-de-la-Tour
Tel: 94.43.70.56
Open: Apr to Sept

Because of the twisty roads, this hideout is for those who don't really care if they ever run down to Saint-Tropez at all and will be content with the country delights of this *provençal* farmhouse near a Roman bridge high above Sainte Maxime. Pool. 6 rooms 400-460 F. 4 suites at 600 F. Meals 210-310 F.

INTERESTING THINGS TO DO

After the beach, or better yet during the low season when heat and crowds are gone, is the time to wander around the old streets of Saint- Tropez, visit its museums, climb up to the **Citadelle**, and watch the fiery red sunset from the ramparts.

MUSEE DE L'ANNONCIADE
Facing the port
Entrance fee: 9.40 F
Hours: May 1-Sept 30: 10-12 and 3-7 pm, rest of the year 10-12 and 2-6 pm. Closed: Nov & Tues

A fine introduction to the Saint-Tropez sites; one hundred impressionist and post-impressionist paintings show the local scene through the eyes of Paul Signac and his friends, Bonnard, Matisse, Dufy or later, Manguin and Van Dongen. Sketches and watercolors by Dunoyer de Segonzac and powerful sculptures by Maillol are shown in the luminous rooms of this XVIth century chapel along with temporary exhibits.

LA PONCHE

Stroll through this old quarter past the **SquareSuffren** tower and the flag-hung **Hôtel de Ville** through narrow streets, past fountains and intriguing doorways, to reach two of the painters' favorite spots: the strand by the old watchtower and the harbor where fishermen mend their nets and compare the day's catch.

THE CHURCH
Rue du Clocher

The open iron campanile on the three-tiered church's clocktower tells of strong *mistral* and *tramontane* winds. In a side-chapel, wooden sculptures show

Saint-Tropez and the original version of his miraculous landing An exceptional *crêche* (manger) is brought out at Christmas.

THE CITADEL

Dominating the city, only peacocks now guard the ramparts that doubled the defenses of the ancient dungeon and towers protecting the Tropezians from attack by sea. Each summer, it becomes the heart of a music festival.

NAVAL MUSEUM

The Citadel
Entrance fee: 9.40 F
Hours: June 15-Sept 15: 10-6pm, the rest of the year: 10-5pm Closed: Thur, Jan 1, Dec 25 and Nov 15 to Dec 15

Ship models, maps and engravings as well as an account of Saint-Tropez' last battle: the Allied landings of 1944.

THE BEACHES AND THE SEA

Where are all the Lovely People? Probably at the beaches, which are a little way outside the town. The scooters and motorbikes churning around as well as all the bicycles, roller skates, and battery-powered skate-boards begin to make sense.

LA BOUILLABAISSE

Only 1 km out of town, but left to the local crowd as is.

PLAGE DES GRANIERS

2 km past the Citadel and the impressive white cemetery that faces the sea. Sailing school at the **Baie des Canoubiers** end.

LES SALINS

4 km via avenue Foch is a smarter choice: it remains the only beach that is still unspoiled. Well, more or less.

TAHITI to PAMPELONNE

By the **Route des Plages** and with several entry points is the mecca with its 6-mile curve of pure sand, the smoothest along the entire Riviera, staked out by dozens of exotically-named concessions renting parasols. Mattress to mattress, bodies – topless, totally nude or clad only in body paint – anoint and offer themselves to the sun in an intense ritual. No time here for dips or sandcastles. For the more active, surfboards and *pédalos* are for rent But the main sport is people-watching. Lunch is taken at the dozens of bars or restaurants, with grilled fish and salads at **TAHITI** (Tel: 94.97.18.02) and *Provençal* fare in the shade and flowers of **CLUB 55,** blvd. Patch (Tel: 94.78.80.14). Sometimes the **MOOREA** and **BAMBOU** are on the insiders' lists but ratings change as notoriously as owners along this golden strip. Expect outrageous prices for the most simple lunch: 130-150 F. Unless you have the gall to bring your own *pan bagnat*.

MONTE CARLO

SBM MONTE-CARLO

J&B

LE METROPOLE

27 × 37 inches

MICHAEL SCARPA - ST. PAUL DE VENCE

VIEWING BY APPOINTEMENT

TEL. : 93.32.60.81

PROVENCE
LAC DE
STE CROIX
N85
LAC DE
ST CASSIEN
D562
DRAGUIGNAN
A8
FRE
ST RA
STE MAXIME
ST TR
VAR
N559
N98

N202
ITALY
ALPES MARITIMES
GRANDE MOYENNE BASSE A8
CORNICHES
MENTON
MONTE-CARLO
MONACO
EZE
BEAULIEU
VILLE FRANCHE
VENCE
ST JENNET
ST PAUL
GRASSE
NICE
CAP FERRAT
D2085
CAGNES
MOUANS SARTOUX
VALBONNE
SOPHIA ANTIPOLIS
MOUGINS
BAIE DES ANGES
JUAN LEEPINS
ANTIBES
CAP D ANTIBES
CANNES
LA NAPOULE
ILE ST MARGUERITE
ILE ST HONORAT
N98
MEDITERRANEAN
COTE D'AZUR

ORDER GUIDES FOR YOURSELF AND YOUR FRIENDS

NAME ....

ADDRESS ....

....

		Per copy	Number of copies	Price
A TOUCH OF **PARIS**	☐	$ 10.00 or FF 70.00 or FS 25.00		
A TOUCH OF **MONACO** and **THE FRENCH RIVIERA**	☐			
A TOUCH OF **GENEVA**	☐			
ALL THREE GUIDES $ 25, FF 175, FS 65	☐			

Contact us directly for larger quantities

TOTAL

Mail your check or money order to:

TRADERS & TRAVELERS / 36, Rue du Colisée 75008 Paris / France

☎ *33 (1) 42.89.49.99 / Telex TRADTOP 643 739*

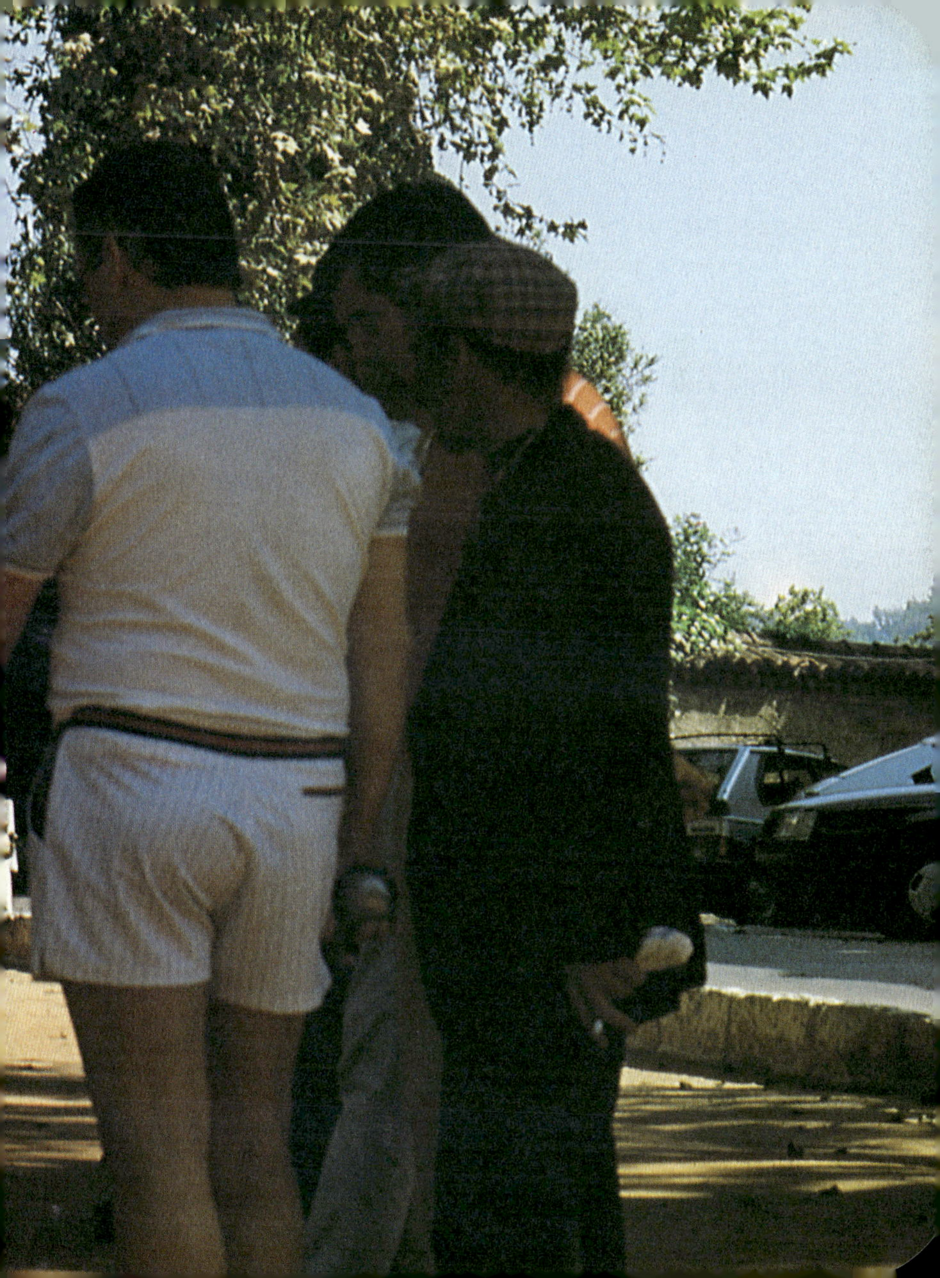

CAFES AND HANG-OUTS

L'ESCALE
Quai Jean-Jaurès
Tel: 94.97.00.63

Remains the place for leisurely drinks in the evening facing the port. An old favorite for its star attractions and fish specialties, and very full in summer.

SENEQUIER
Tel: 94.97.00.90

LE GORILLE
Tel: 94.97.03.93

Seemingly reserved for the bronzed and beautiful, but also quayside vantage points for seeing and being seen and capturing the whole essence of Saint-Tropez. During high season, many who *know* prefer to turn up here for morning *café* and *croissants* than the traditional *apéritifs*.

CAFE DES ARTS
Place des Lices
Tel: 94.97.02.25

Pastis in what used to be an authentic village *café* with a shabby charm, is always "in". The restaurant at the back serves *Provençal daubes* and *gratins* at reasonable prices (all is relative) 130F-140 F.

BISTROT DES LICES
3, place des Lices
Tel: 94.97.29.00

Has a popular piano bar that serves as a good rendezvous before attacking the discos. (also serves meals, 120-250 F)

NANO
4, rue Sybille
Tel: 94.97.01.66

Young, trendy even gay atmosphere in this bar-cum- restaurant open all year round. 180-200 F.

CAFE DES ARTS
BOULES

SOMETHING TO TAKE HOME

FACONNABLE
6, rue François Sibilli
Tel: 94.97.29.98

BARCLAY
20, rue Allard
Tel: 94.97.02.05

Both cater to the yacht clientele with fine, classic menswear.

GIANNI VERSACE
30, rue François Sibilli
Tel: 94.97.42.96

More up to the minute.

JEAN CLAUDE J3
Rue de la Ponche

Original leather clothes.

PEAU D'ANE
3, place de l'Hôtel de Ville

For superb bathing suits.

VACHON
MIC MAC
CHOSES
Quai Suffren
Quai Jean-Jaurès

Offer T-shirts, beachwear and the slinkiest pants. You may find the same in your hometown department store under the same labels but they are more irresistible here.

HERMES
CARTIER
5, rue de la Ponche
Tel: 94.97.06.78

The preppie staples: eternal scarves, bags and essential *Musts*.

FRANCOIS
8, rue de la Ponche
Tel: 94.97.25.75

There are several around the area where you'll find jangly junk jewelry and ear-rings.

SOULEIADO
Hôtel Byblos

Irresistible cottons in old *Provençal* block prints for house and leisure wear.

RONDINI
Rue Clemenceau

Tropezian thonged-leather sandals that have replaced the barefoot look.

GRAIN DE SEL
24, rue Allard
Tel: 94.97.01.34

House linens and gifts with a difference.

JEU D'OMBRES
28, rue Citadelle
Tel: 94.97.07.04

Unusual lamps and shades.

MILLE SABORDS
8, rue des Commerçants
Tel: 94.97.07.79
Kids' stuff for the young nautical crowd.

EXCURSIONS AROUND SAINT-TROPEZ

All around the Saint-Tropez peninsula, blissfully free from railway, highways or sophisticated seafront promenades, roads wind through dark woods, scented *garrigues* or along the vineyards to reach cool hill-sites where villages once braved the Saracens or were held by them.

RAMATUELLE

The road climbs up past the chapel dedicated to Sainte Anne (a longtime pilgrimage-spot). Make a detour to the tip of the barren **Cap Camarat** to see the view, or continue to the highest point: the 3 ruined windmills at the **Moulins de Paillas**. You might stop for lunch at the bistrot terraces of hilltop...

GASSIN

...or at the nearby inn of **La Verdoyante** (Tel: 94.56.16.23, Open: mid-March to Nov) which pleasantly serves *Provençal* dishes for a moderate 100 F. Celebrate this find with a Château-Minuty rosé from the neighbouring vineyards of **Château Minuty** (Tel: 94.56.12.09) or like the **Château-Barbeyrolles** (Tel: 94.56.33 58), the **Domaine de Bertaud** (Tel: 94.56.16.83), the **Château de Pampelonne** (Tel: 94.56.32 04) and most of the wine producers in the area, welcome visitors to its cellars during working-hours to taste wines that grow on this flinty terrain. The mild maritime climate is particularly favorable to light rosé wines. Some interesting reds as well.

PORT GRIMAUD

On the gulf of Saint-Tropez, a modern marina created by architect François Spoerry on reclaimed marshland, a Saint-Tropez reinvented, with a touch of Venice. Boats are anchored at the foot of the gardens, and canals and bridges link the houses. Pleasure and excursion boats putt-putt around, and groceries and newspapers are delivered by boat. Fun to explore on foot or by *coche d'eau*. Great view from the oecumenical church tower. Stop by **La Tartane** (Tel: 94.56.38.32) for a quayside lunch (170-250 F) and visit the boutiques for house gifts, beach-togs, and handicraft goods. A good hotel is **La Giraglia** (Tel: 94.56.3l.33) which has its own beach and pool. Open: end March to Oct 1. 48 rooms 102O-1150 F.

GRIMAUD

This high-perched fief is crowned by the impressive ruins of a castle built by the Grimaldis in the Middle Ages, embellished by the Castellanes and torn down during the French Revolution. After roaming the old streets, you might try **Les Santons,** long a star choice for its *terrine d'agneau aux aubergines* (from 290-380 F) or **Le Pâtissier du Château** for unusual pies served on the terrace.

COGOLIN

A small but bustling industrious center that makes briar pipes and turns reeds from the marshes into porch furniture and fishing rods. **Les Tapis de Cogolin** at 98, boulevard Louis Blanc is a factory outlet and decorator's choice for high-pile rugs. The **Domaine des Garcinières** (Tel: 94.56.02.85 or 94.56.09.25) and the **Domaine de Saint Maur** (Tel: 94.56.09.25) are both well worth a cellar visit.

LA FOUX

To return to Saint-Tropez, you must inevitably pass this notorious crossroads. If it is clogged with traffic, it's a good excuse to stop at the wine cooperative **Les Maîtres Vignerons de la Presqu'île de Saint-Tropez** (Tel: 94.56.32.04) for a comparison test while you wait for traffic to ease off. Open during working hours. Closed Saturday afternoons and Sundays.

SAINTE-MAXIME

Just across the bay, this pretty resort has traditional amenities like a promenade and casino, and can be reached either by regular boats from Saint-Tropez or by road. It has a **Phonograph Museum** (Tel: 94.96.50.52) with vintage music boxes, pianolas and record players that came before juke-boxes or flippers. Open: May l to Sept 3O, 9 am-7 pm. Entrance fee: 9 F. Closed on Tuesdays and some holidays. The **Calidianus** (Tel: 94.96.23.21) has 27 quiet, pleasant rooms at around 330 F. Pool. Tennis. There is also a 9-hole golf course at Beauvallon – the nearest one to Saint-Tropez.

FREJUS

A Roman garrison after Caesar came and conquered, and the ruins prove it: arenas where bullfights are held, an aqueduct and the statue of a patron goddess. An unexpected delight in this busy seaside town is the Cathedral's medieval cloister around a romantic courtyard overgrown with pink laurel. Closed from noon to 2 pm and Tuesdays.

A LONGER EXCURSION: HAUTE PROVENCE AND THE WINE COUNTRY

Within less than one hundred kilometers of Saint-Tropez, past the commercial artery of the N7 and the Autoroute, are departmental roads that climb from the flat fertile plain that separates the coastal mountain ranges from the high plateaus of the Alps of **Haute Provence**. They wind past vineyards planted in geometric pattern on the red soil, terraced *restanques* of silvery olive trees and through forests of scrub, whiteoak and pines. Fragances of lavender, wild rosemary, thyme or golden broom are pervasive, outcrops of sheer white rocks dramatic. In the distance are the layered blues of the **Massif des Maures** hiding Saint-Tropez and the sea. Within a few hours, you can visit abbeys and castles, markets and craft centres, and acquaint yourself with a few great *rosés.* The rosy shade is not obtained by a mix of white and red as one might think but from the length of time the grapes remain in the vats where the pigments in the grape-skin color the juice in as little as 24 hours. Provençal wines, a gift of the Greeks, religiously cultivated by medieval monks, have long been underestimated, but are now being improved. Producers have worked hard to better them so that they can now age and travel. The higher altitudes, a different soil and a harsher climate yield the heady red wines (one third of the production) that go with the wild game the locals hunt with such determination.

THE UPPER VAR

LES ARCS-SUR-ARGENS

Considers itself the capital of the **Côtes de Provence**. Though these wines can be also be white or red, about 60 percent of the production is the *rosé* that suits light summer meals and sea fare or the many combinations of tomatoes, eggplant and squash – from *ratatouille* to *provençal gratins.* Try them at restaurants, bring them along on picnics or sample them in wine cellars to discover your own favorites. The **Syndicat des Vins Côtes de Provence** (Tel: 94.73.31.01) just before Les Arcs offers wines from 400 regional producers. Nearby, you can find **Château Saint-Roseline** (Tel: 94.73.32.57), a *cru classé* , also known for strong reds. In the midst of the vineyards, you can also visit the **Chapel Saint-Roseline**, what remains of a medieval abbey. Open: July 1 to Sept 30 on Wednesdays, Saturdays and Sundays from 3:30 to 6:30 pm. The rest of the year on Wednesdays and Sundays from 2:30 pm to 4:30 pm. Beside its baroque altarpiece, there are works by Chagall and other modern artists illustrating the legend of the sainted abbess.

VILLECROZE

A waterfall and strange grotto strongholds carved into the cliffs in Gothic times can be seen every day from June 15 to Sept 30 from 9 to 12 and 1:30 to 7:30 pm. The rest of the year visits are limited to Wednesdays, Saturdays and Sundays, from 10 am-Noon and 2-5 pm. On the way, stop at the **Domaine Saint-Jean** for wines nurtured with no chemical fertilizers, no pesticides or herbicides and filtered by the most natural processes and as a result this rosé has a crystal-clear salmon tint. Thenearby **Domaine de Thuerry** also has wines served in local bistrots and restaurants. In the same area, the **Bastide de Tourtour** (Tel: 94.70.57.30 telex 70827) Open: 15 Feb to 15 Nov, for an elegant stay in a delightful situation close to the attractive village and its massive church. 26 rooms. Pool. 460-800 F. Meals 190-270 F. The **Auberge Saint-Pierre** (Tel: 94.70.57.17) in the landscaped development of Saint Pierre de Tourtour, has a pool and terrace amidst grassy pastures. Open: Apr 1 to Oct 15. 15 rooms 230-260 F. **Les Chênes Verts** (Tel: 4.70.55.06) is a one-star restaurant. Closed from Jan 1 to Feb 15, Sunday evenings and Mondays. Meals 220-320 F including wine.

AUPS

In markets around, watch out for locally produced olive oil and **Ferme de Tourtour** products: exclusive and unusual pâtés (*grives* or *sanglier*), potted *daubes* and *anchoiades* to take home a taste of Provence. The leisurely life of the *arrière pays* depends much on shopping for local produce, meeting friends in the local café, inviting them home to share your finds: a *pain aux olives*, a salad of tomatoes, anchovies with more Nyons olives and some goat cheese.

SALERNES

For typical *provençal* décor, this is the place to shop for outstanding ceramics. Small factories and master craftsmen are lined along the main road to Draguignan and have more outlets in town. Most of the prettiest hand-decorated tiles are made only to order in small batches. Expect delays and many compliments on the result. Earthenware is shaped into distinctive *tians* that could be used to toss a huge buffet salad or built in as small washbasins. There are pots and bowls, of course, as well as traditional reddish terra-cotta *tomettes* and large floor-tiles. Among many others, **Polidori** and the **Ateliers de la Baume**, turn out traditional or unusual pottery with tender loving care.

CHATEAU D'ENTRECASTEAUX

Tel: 94.04.43.95
Hours: April-Sept, 10 am-8 pm
Oct-March, 10 am-6 pm

A rock-based fortress rebuilt in the XVIIth century as a pleasure castle above a garden designed by Lenôtre. The herb-spiced local dishes and lavish summer entertaining were praised by Mme de Sévigné who came here to visit her daughter, Mme de Grignan. Practically abandoned since the Revolution, the present owners have restored it themselves with loving care and make the castle relive with exhibits and concerts. A master bedroom and adjoining marble bathroom have been turned into a sumptuous *chambre d'hôte* worthy of the Sun King himself. The owner, of Scottish descent, also makes a distinctive orange marmalade laced with whisky. It's on sale along with wines and local specialties.

ABBAYE DU THORONET

Tel: 94.73.87.13
Closed: Noon-2 pm and some public holidays

Virtually hidden in a wooded valley, the austere buildings have not changed since Cistercian monks and itinerant stone cutters teamed up to raise them in the XIIth century. The proportions of the vast church, the dormitory and cloister are impressive for sheer simplicity. From here, an attractive but rather twisting route returns to Grimaud and Saint-Tropez via **La Garde-Freinet**, once a Saracen stronghold (today a Parisian one), replete with craftshops.

Mavis Guinard

MAVIS GUINARD, an American journalist and translator, divides her time between Switzerland and the South of France. Her features on both areas have appeared in the "International Herald Tribune".

PIZZA
POULETS
A EMPORTER
SNACK

7
EATING OUT ON THE RIVIERA: A TASTE OF A GREAT ART

173 | Eating with the Gods
176 | Local Cooking
179 | Good Places to Eat

EATING OUT

For over 150 years, the chefs of France, Europe and the world have been drawn to the Riviera. They have come to cook for the rich and famous, or to perfect their art under the guidance of the great names of French cuisine. They have opened restaurants whose names are known the other end of the globe, and have created dishes that are part of the standard repertoire of millions of restaurants worldwide.

Settling in this sunny region by the sea, they found cooking traditions that were already well-developed: *la cuisine provençale* with its aromatic herbs, and dishes reminiscent of old Provençal farm-houses; la *cuisine niçoise*, with the strong tangy flavour of the back-streets and old harbour of Nice; and other *cuisines* influenced by the Italians arriving from the East and South. The newcomers could not help but be influenced, and today, in the restaurants of the great chefs of the coast, you can still taste the rough charm of these dishes. Roger Vergé, one of the greatest chefs of our generation, calls it *la cuisine du soleil*.

On the Riviera today, you can taste this *cuisine* not only in its new sophisticated form, but also in the unpretentious restaurants of villages and backstreets, where families continue to cook in the traditional way they have always cooked.

You can also find restaurants to represent every region of France: the creamy dishes of Normandy, the solid fare of Alsace, the sophisticated sauces of Lyon, the rich earthy food of the South West. The rest of the world is well represented: lots of Italian restaurants, some Spanish, a handful Russian, two Hungarian, and assorted Arab and oriental. In Nice, a single street boasts over a dozen Vietnamese restaurants. There is a famous Danish restaurant near Saint Paul-de-Vence, and even an Irish restaurant in the Old Town of Nice (unless it has been closed once again for its night-time revelling!).

There are also restaurants of all styles, from the simple and homelike to the elegant and pretentious. There are restaurants on beaches, in shady squares, in palaces, castles, churches and cellars. There are restaurants alongside busy highways, on mule-tracks, on clifftops, and in the depths of forests. There are more restaurants than you can imagine, and still more new ones opening every year.

Visitors to the Riviera sometimes wonder if they will be served poor food and indifferent wine, fearing that the mass of tourists to the region will have brought the standards down. Not to worry. This is France, and there is no nation on earth that is more critical and demanding of its restaurateurs, and even in a good location a poor restaurant will never survive.

Nor would the restaurateurs want it any other way. The cooks and serving-staff of the Riviera take pride in the quality of their food in the face of the most adverse circumstances. In the middle of August, with all the tables filled, and more people arriving by the minute, the headwaiter or cook of a successful restaurant are attentive to every table, stop to talk about the meal to explain why a dish was cooked the way it was and to check the service. This is not only a profession, but an art. On the Riviera, you will see some of the best artists around.

EATING WITH THE GODS: GREAT (AND RATHER EXPENSIVE) RESTAURANTS

The Riviera has more than its share of great restaurants. The Gault-Millau *Guide de la Côte d'Azur,* which is required reading for any serious gourmet, lists five "very greats", **Le Chantecler**, **L'Oasis**, **Le Moulin de Mougins**, **La Bonne Auberge** and **Le Royal Gray**. These restaurants and their chefs are spoken of in hushed whispers. The Moulin de Mougins, run by Roger Vergé, one of the high priests of French cuisine, is a place of pilgrimage, and the meal a sacrament. An expensive sacrament, as the bill rarely falls below 600 F per person.

These chefs are stars, as well-known as football-players, and better-known than most great writers. Their rise or fall in the estimation of Michelin or Gault et Millau is followed with bated breath. The former awards stars (one to three) as a mark of esteem, the latter *toques* (or chefs hats), four *toques* being the highest. Characteristically, all French people will claim to be in violent disagreement with the judgements of either guide, but in fact there is little dispute about where to go to get a really superb meal.

Another wonderful thing about the Riviera is the number of restaurants that are not in the ranks of stardom, but which are truly excellent. In the 300 F price-area (wine included), you can get a meal you won't forget, served with flair and imagination. The Riviera is particularly lucky in this respect, and a visitor could eat top-class cooking for a month, without dining twice in the same restaurant. In his pilgrimage from restaurant to restaurant, the visitor would also see some of the pleasantest locations a restaurant could wish for, and some of the most dramatic: under the palm trees, overlooking the blue Mediterranean, in shady valleys and on the peaks of mountains. Perfect food in a perfect landscape... what other pleasures could you ask for?

CANNES

LE MOULIN DE MOUGINS

424, chemin du Moulin
Quartier Notre Dame de Vie
MOUGINS
Tel: 93.75.78.24
Closed: Thur lunch & Mon

Many of the other chefs of the region were trained by Roger Vergé, a genial wizard who is constantly launching new projects and ideas. The menu is a inventive, and the restaurant offers up to 50 new dishes every year.

L'OASIS

Rue Jean-Honoré-Carle
LA NAPOULE
Tel: 93.49.95.52
Closed: Mon evening & Tues

Chef Louis Outhier has managed the remarkable feat of linking French and Oriental cuisine, in a series of extraordinary creations which are all his own.
Around 600 F.

LE ROYAL GRAY

Hotel Gray d'Albion
6, rue des Etats Unis
CANNES
Tel: 93.99.04.59
Closed: Mon lunch & Sun

The Gray d'Albion hotel only opened in 1981, but the management made a smart move in selecting

Jacques Chibois as Chef. In only a few years, this restaurant has earned recognition as perhaps the finest table in Cannes. At festival-time, it is the haunt of filmstars, and it is increasingly recommended by local gourmets. The cooking is delicate, with a light Provençal flavour. Around 500 F.

L'AMANDIER

Place du Commandant-Lamy
MOUGINS
Tel: 93.90.00.91
Closed: Sat lunch & Wed

Very classy cooking at very reasonable prices, under the supervision of Francis Chauveau. Wonderful view from the terrace, across the hills to the Alps. Around 350 F.

LE CAGNARD

Rue du Pontis-Long
Haut de Cagnes
CAGNES-SUR-MER
Tel: 93.20.73.21
Closed: Thur lunch

A restaurant in a true medieval setting, with staircases, arches and vaults, decorated with imagination and style. Chef Jean-Yves Johanny has plenty of imagination too, and this restaurant is generally considered to be on the way to the top. Around 350 F.

LA RESERVE

91, boulevard de la Plage
CAGNES-SUR-MER
Tel: 93.31.00.17
Closed: Sat dinner, Sun, July and Aug

Not only does Chef Loulou Bertho close for the weekend, but he is also closed July and August! A pity for the summer visitor, but a good indication of where his priorities lie. Famous not only for the fish, fresh from the boats, but also for the quality of the meat: almost worth changing your holiday-plans to be here when he's open. Around 280 F.

NICE

CHATEAU DE LA CHEVRE D'OR

EZE VILLAGE (between Nice and Monaco, on the Moyenne Corniche)
Tel: 93.41.12.12
Closed: Wed

Eat there in daylight, and ask (well in advance) for a table with a view. The *Château* hangs on a precipice dropping several hundred feet to the sea, and you can see way over to the Esterel behind Cannes. The view won't distract you from the superb meal, neatly and elegantly served under the supervision of Mr Ingold himself. Around 350 F.

LE CHANTECLER
Hotel Negresco
37, Promenade des Anglais
NICE
Tel: 93.88.39.51

The Chef is Jacques Maximin, elected *Premier Grand Chef de France* a couple of years ago, and going from strength to strength. He is a master of *natural* cooking, a *virtuose* in the words of Gault Millau, making use of the flavours of each ingredient, and even proposing a menu composed entirely of cooked vegetables. From 700.

MONACO

DOMINIQUE LE STANC
18, boulevard des Moulins
MONACO
Tel: 93.50.63.37
Closed: Sun and Mon

Definitely the best restaurant in Monaco, under the supervision of one of the younger chefs around, Dominique Le Stanc, who is 27 years old. Very original decor, including an unusual collection of antique dolls. Around 350 F.

LOCAL COOKING

In many restaurants of the Riviera, the menu will advertise dishes labelled *Niçoise* or *à la Provençale.* In most cases, this says nothing about the origin of the recipe, and merely indicates that the dish will probably include tomatoes, peppers, olives, and even anchovies — the ingredients most associated with the South of France.

In some restaurants, however, local cooking is truly being revived, after decades of domination by Paris and Lyon. Many elegant restaurants now offer *soupe de poisson, agneau de Sisteron,* and other dishes that used to be considered suitable only for fishermen and peasants.

Jacques Médecin, mayor of Nice, has himself written a *Niçois* cookbook, and family-style restaurants in the backstreets of Nice, which have cooked *Niçois* food for workers and students for generations, are now being invaded by gourmets in smart clothes. Even the *traiteurs* (delicatessens) who would previously have disdained any adjective except *Lyonnais*, now display *spécialités locales* in their elegant windows.

However, the cooking of the South, though rough and simple, is not so easy to imitate. *Soupe de poisson* takes a full day to make, a day of back-breaking work, shelling the shellfish, cleaning, straining and mixing. Some restaurants take short cuts; others buy it frozen. But if ever you find the real thing, you will never forget it. To taste *soupe de poisson à la Niçoise* is reason enough to come to the Riviera.

In the list below, we have included restaurants who have come to a satisfactory agreement with the local fishermen, and really serve fresh fish daily. This assurance of eating the inhabitants of the nearest bay justifies the classification of local, even though fresh fish well served surpasses any boundaries or classifications.

SAINT TROPEZ

LEI MOUSCARDINS
at the end of the harbour
SAINT-TROPEZ
Tel: 94.97.01.53

Offers a dominating view over the bay. For an authentic *bouillabaisse* with no unneeded frills, a saffron-spiced broth, big chunks of fresh red mullet and rock fish, *croûtons* and tasty *rouille*. Around 230 F.

LA RAMADE
Rue du Temple
SAINT-TROPEZ
Tel: 94.97.00.15

A real bistrot, frequented by the local *tropéziens* , and serving excellent fresh fish, for the good reason that the patron is a fisherman. Try the *sardines farcies* and the *soupe au fenouil*. From 200 to 250 F.

FIFINE
Rue Suffren
SAINT-TROPEZ
TEL: 94.97.03.90

A born cook lords over a small restaurant unfortunately overrun by tourists who couldn't care less. But, on order, she will prepare a classic *bouillabaisse* to rave about.
Around 200 F.

CANNES

CHEZ ARISTIDE
46, avenue de Lérins
THEOULE SUR MER
Tel: 93.49.96.13
Closed: Mon

The menus in this excellent fish-restaurant vary according to the day's catch. Very reasonably priced for the quality. Around 150 F.

CHEZ FREDERIC
Island of ST. HONORAT
Tel: 93.48.66.88
Closed: evenings

Frédéric serves *La célèbre langouste Frédéric* (his famous lobster) which would taste good in any setting. On this lovely little island, on the restaurant terrace with its lovely view, it is nothing less than delicious. Reserve in advance. Can easily climb to 250 F or over.

LA MERE BESSON
13, rue des Frères-Pradignac
CANNES
Tel: 93.39.59.24
Open 'til 10 pm
Dinner only July & Aug

Long popular with festival-goers, this restaurant goes on even without *la Mère Besson* herself. Provençal decor and cuisine (the *aïoli* served on Fridays is considered one of the best of the region. Try also the *salade niçoise)* . Service is friendly and often slow in this always packed house. Around 200 F *à la carte.*

AUBERGE DE LA CHEVRE D'OR
Place Chauve
PEYMEINADE
Tel: 93.60.54.22
Closed: Mon

A "get away from it all" kind of place, in a little village near Grasse. Grilled meats, Provençal specialties, and also dishes from the South-West. Around 120 F.

LA FARIGOULE
15, avenue Henri Isnard
VENCE
Tel: 93.58.01.27

Good Provençal cooking in a family establishment that has been run for the last 26 years by Mme Gastaud. Covered terrace in the summer season. Very modest prices for local wines and such regional specialties as *sardines à l'escabèche, osso bucco à la niçoise* and *lapin à la farigoule.* Around 100 F.

LE BELIER NOIR
VIEUX VILLAGE DE CARROS
Tel: 93.29.10.49

A real country inn, next to the town hall in the beautiful village of Carros (not to be confused with Carros-le-Neuf in the valley below). Lamb and *Estouffade de boeuf* served very simply by *la patronne* , on a terrace overlooking the valley of the Var river. Around 100 F (take the menu).

NICE

POUPON ET MARINETTE: LE RENDEZ-VOUS DES SPORTIFS
120, boulevard de la Madeleine
NICE
Tel: 93.86.21.39

An unpretentious restaurant, and traditional *Niçois* cooking at its best, with a homely atmosphere and an impressive list of famous clients. Help yourself to big baskets of fresh salads and raw vegetable with anchovy sauce, then, if you're feeling adventurous, choose a *Stockfisch* (a very unusual fish stew), or a *Menon aux poivrons* (tender goat with red peppers). Some nice local wines, including Bellet, the only wine produced in the Nice region. From 120 to 150 F.

NISSA SOCCA
5, rue Sainte Réparate (just by the cathedral)
NICE
Tel. 93.80.18.35
Closed: Sun evening & Mon

Socca is the flat cake you sometimes see being sold in the streets of the old town, made from chick-pea flour, and is something of a symbol for the rough and friendly taste of Niçois cooking. Nissa Socca, a tiny little restaurant, serves the real thing (even though the managers are Corsican!), including delicious aubergine and courgette fritters, and fresh home-made pasta. As little as 100 F.

GOOD PLACES TO EAT

Here is a small selection from among the many excellent restaurants scattered along the Riviera coast. These restaurants are not necessarily famous, but may be recommendations passed around by locals, and many of them charge prices way below those for meals of comparable quality in Britain or the States.

However, there are restaurants still cheaper than these, providing meals that are *corrects* (a term of real praise in France), or, if you prefer, good honest food, cooked in the French style. You can find these restaurants in any town, in almost any street. Most towns also have a restaurant-area, a neighbourhood where the eating-houses are spread before you like a menu, where you can spend a very pleasant half-hour wandering from restaurant to restaurant, reading the mouth-watering descriptions of what they have to offer. In Cannes, for example, climb the **rue du Suquet**, the narrow street winding up behind the port; in Antibes, stroll down the **rue James Close** (in the old town) and across the **place Nationale**; in Nice, start at the **Cours Saleya** and head inland; in Villefranche, go down to the sea-front.

For each restaurant, we have given approximate prices (per person), which assume that you will tend to choose a fixed menu (usually a smart decision), though not necessarily the cheapest, and that you won't splash out on the most expensive wines, but may include little extras like a drink before dinner. In some restaurants where fresh fish is served or soufflés made to order, keep an eye on the price-column and a tight rein on your guests, or you may be paying two-star prices after all!

SAINT-TROPEZ

LA ROMANA
Chemin des Conquettes
SAINT-TROPEZ
Tel: 94.97.15.50

The French interpretation of an Italian restaurant ranges from the sublime to the appalling. This one is at the top end. Even the pizzas are excellent in this unpretentious and friendly eating-house, frequented by both stars and locals. Has the reputation of catering to the loveliest girls in *Saint-Trop.* 170 to 200 F.

CANNES

LA CHUNGA
72, La Croisette
CANNES
Tel: 93.94.11.29

Fashionable, flashy and smooth, and always a big success. Located near the Martinez Hotel. In the piano bar, the action goes on all night, while in the restaurant, music and candlelight, on a terrace overlooking the Bay of Cannes. Around 250 F, but you'll be tempted to spend more.

LE RESTAU DES ARTS
6, avenue Boucherie
CANNES
Tel: 93.39.22.38
Closed: Tue

Essential to reserve, at any time of year, in this friendliest of Paris-style bistros, with charming low-key service from the two gay brothers who run it. An undemanding restaurant for a relaxing evening among friends. Located in the Suquet. From 130 to 170 F.

FEU FOLLET
Place de la Mairie
MOUGINS
Tel: 93.90.03.74.

Run by the same family as the **Relais de Mougins** across the road (the Surmains), but about half the price and considerably more than half as good. Simple and unpretentious, with a lovely view. As little as 120 F.

CHEZ NOU-NOU
Bord de Mer (Cannes end)
GOLFE JUAN
Tel: 93.63.71.73

Yes, you can get a good meal at a restaurant on the beach. This is the most famous on this stretch of coast, and though the service is sometimes a bit slow, it's worth waiting for. Fish is the specialty (of course). Around 150 F.

ENTRE COUR ET JARDIN

Montée de la Bourgade
HAUT DE CAGNES
Tel: 93.20.72.27
Closed: Mon

The name suggests sunny court-yards and gardens. Even though it has neither, they still manage to convey that image, with tasteful wall-paintings and delicate cooking (*salade tiède de lotte aux fonds d'artichaut, magret de canard au cidre,* and very, very nice desserts). Exceptional quality for the price, though the service is sometimes a little confused. Around 150 F.

ANTIBES

ESTEREL PLAGE

Bord de Mer (sea-front)
JUAN-LES-PINS
Tel: 93.61.04.18
Open every day in the season.
Closed: in winter.

One of the better beach restaurants at Juan-les-Pins, a resort not usually noted for wonderful cuisine. Around 120 F.

LE CABESTAN

Boulevard de la Garoupe
CAP d'ANTIBES
Tel: 93.61.77.70

A lovely view of the bay of La Garoupe, and very high quality service. Specialised in fishdishes, including their extra- ordinary *Poisson en croûte de sel* (served in a salt jacket!). Over 300 F.

LA MARGUERITE

11 rue Sadi Carnot
ANTIBES
Tel: 93.34.08.27
Closed: Sun evenings & Mon

One of the best addresses in Antibes, in a banal setting stylishly decorated, not far from the Port Vauban. The cuisine is definitely *gastronomique*, including *estouffade d'agneau et surflan de courgettes* and *mousseline de coquilles Saint Jacques à la crême d'échalottes*. The atmosphere is rather precious, not to say old-maidish, but you can't complain about the prices. Around 200 F.

VENCE

LA GOUSSE D'AIL

7, Ramparts Ouest
ST. PAUL-DE-VENCE
Tel: 93.32.50.48
Closed: Wed & winter

Jacques and Evelyne have opened a sorely needed restaurant in Saint Paul – one where you can eat well without draining the pocket-book or weighing down on the digestion. The menu includes *poussin au nid* and *escalope de saumon frais*. The perfect interlude on your walk around the city ramparts. About 140 F.

L'AUBERGE DES TEMPLIERS
39, avenue Joffre
VENCE
Tel: 93.58.06.05
Closed: Sun evening & Mon

A garden and a rustic dining-room, with a cheerful welcome and attentive service. *Gateau de St.Pierre à l'estragon* and *carré d'agneau au poivre vert*. The 90 F menu is excellent value. Around 120 F.

NICE

PETITE MAISON FERRIER
Corner of Rue de l'Opéra and Rue Saint François de Paule
NICE
Tel: 93.92.59.59
Closed: Sun

An elegant setting in the old town of Nice, a friendly welcome and an imaginative young chef. Open all day, (serves good pastries at tea-time) and features two gourmet menus in the evening (130 F and 180 F), including *brouillade aux truffes* and *fricassée de homard à l'ail doux*. About 170 F.

CARPACCIO
Promenade des Marinières
VILLEFRANCHE SUR MER
Tel: 93.01.72.97
Closed: Tues

A big and unpretentious *brasserie* overlooking the bay of Villefranche, serving lots of good honest food, with a fine selection of ice-creams to top it off. Good place to take the family. From 100 to 140 F.

MONACO

EDEN TERRAZZA
Port du Cap d'Ail
just outside MONACO
Tel: 93.78.39.43
Closed: Mon.

At the water's edge of Monaco's newly constructed harbour, a luxurious restaurant with fish specialties. Special lunch-time menu at 150 F. Otherwise, from 200 to 250 F.

LE BEC ROUGE (LE P'TIT BEC)
11, avenue de Grande Bretagne
MONACO
Tel: 93.30.74.91

An excellent address remembered by many faithful (and famous) clients. Classical cuisine of excellent quality and freshness, including *foie gras frais de maison, gratin de langouste* and *loup du pays*. 150 F menu at lunchtime only. Between 200 & 300 F *à la carte*.

POLPETTA
2, rue Paradis
MONACO
Tel: 93.50.67.84
Closed: Tues

A warm welcome and a relaxed atmosphere in this newly-decorated and very popular Italian restaurant. Pasta, risotto and sea-food salads at reasonable prices – for Monaco! Around 130 F.

David Ward-Perkins

DAVID WARD-PERKINS is a freelance writer and journalist working on the French Riviera. His special fields are high-tech business, education and tourism.

8
RIVIERA NIGHTLIFE

186	Nightlife: Ballet
	Opera
	Concert Music
	Festivals
	Pop and Rock
	Cabarets
	Theatres
	Cinemas
	Racing
192	Casinos
196	Nightclubs and Discos
196	Bars, Piano-Bars and Cafés

The *Côte d'Azur*, with its subtle blend of wealth, elegance and hedonistic pleasures, exercises an irresistible pull on everyone, from temperamental tennis champions like Boris Becker to seductive screen goddesses like Brigitte Bardot.

Its image as the playground of Princes, pop-stars and millionaires, whose wealth goes even deeper than their sun-tans, has become a little tarnished in recent years. But even though the camping-car brigade has been invading the privileged enclaves of the jet-set, there is still plenty of room along the Riviera's privileged coastline for all those fun-lovers out for a good time.

On the balmy moon-lit Mediterranean nights, the coast is alive to the sound of popping champagne corks. Each town has its own version of the high life. The bustling port of Saint-Tropez is for the trendy night revelers; Cannes, which houses many conferences, caters to a more professional category of party goers — especially during the film festival, when the sunlights stay on until dawn; after-hours in Nice tend to be more sedate, but do retain a definite Gallic flavor. As for pristine Monaco, it is preferable to have a golden wallet, but then again, this is the place to frequent if you wish to rub elbows with royalty out on the town. It is the Principality's proud boast that a woman can safely wear a million dollars worth of jewels, unless of course she is out "to catch a thief". Many a night, there is a Duchess or a Dame who can be seen putting it to the test.

In Monaco, the social season begins with the **Rose Ball** (in March) and lasts until the **Red Cross Ball** (in August). If you are in town at that time, it is worth visiting the **Hôtel de Paris** at *apéritif* hour to see the *crème de la crème* glittering.

Ballet

The delicately ornate **Salle Garnier** in the Casino was home of Diaghilev's Russian ballets at the turn of the century. They first put Monaco on the cultural map. Now Princess Caroline has brought to life the dream of her late mother, Princess Grace, to recreate the Monte Carlo ballets and set up a new company of 34 dancers. It costs "no more than a football team," says the Princess, and they are a lot lighter on their feet.

Opera

There are also some magnificent productions in the **Salle Garnier** at Monaco. Although a delightful setting, it is small and tickets are snapped up by border-raiding parties of opera-hungry Italians.

Nice also has the delightful **Opera House** with a more adventurous program. They also make use of the **Acropolis**, the new Convention center, which has superb acoustics and facilities for staging grand productions with big names like Placido Domingo.

Concert Music

Still on the classical side of life, during the summer there are concerts in the romantic setting of the court of honour at the **Prince's Palace** by the **Monte-Carlo Philharmonic Orchestra** which is establishing something of an international reputation for itself.

The prestigious **Orchestre Régional Provence Alpes — Côte d'Azur** also has a full program around the region — in particular at the **Palais des Festivals** in Cannes where they are based.

Festivals

The most famous of them all is the **Cannes Film Festival** — usually held in May. This ritzy resort then becomes a place of fantasy, indulgence and excess fit for any B movie. The posing starlets, posturing producers and a handful of film tycoons are pursued by a posse of pressmen 3,000 strong. It's almost impossible to see any of the films or join in the fun of the champagne receptions unless you are officially accredited to the festival. However, you can join the throng of beautiful people milling along the *Croisette*, looking for the stars or waiting to be discovered.

Equally dazzling to the eyes is the **International Fireworks Festival**, which helps the summer take off with a bang in Monte Carlo.

A more tuneful way to pass the hazy summer nights is at the **Cimiez Jazz Festival** in Nice, where, among the Roman ruins, you can swing along to some of the greats of the Jazz world, including Fats Domino, Lionel Hampton and Buddy Rich. Further along the coast in the shaded setting of *La Pinède*, the **Antibes/Juans-les-Pins Jazz Festival** doubles up on the pleasure. Past headliners have included Jimmy Cliff and Miles Davis.

Pop and Rock

To show the old can live with the new, the last remnants of the Roman arenas at **Fréjus (Les Arènes)** are regularly rocked by the beat of pop supergroups. The most accessible place, however, is the **Théâtre de Verdure** in Nice. The canvas covering used in the winter is taken down during the summer so the fans can bop away under the stars to the sounds of Mike Oldfield, Sting, Culture Club, et al.

Cabarets

The best cabaret-shows are in Monaco — **Le Cabaret du Casino** (Reservations: 93.50.69.31), which has slick, high-quality American-style shows with dinner-dance and occasional big-name stars. The **Folie Russe** at the Hôtel Loews (Tel: 93.50.65.00) is a ritzy-glitzy-type of show, with particular emphasis on the nubile young dancers. Prices are on the steep side.

Theatres

For those whose French is up to it, there is the **Princess Grace Theatre** in Monaco or the **Nouveau Théâtre de Nice**, which has a more experimental program and is currently directed by one of France's best actors, Jacques Weber. For a more relaxed atmosphere there are a handful of café-theatres along the coast.

Cinemas

Nice and Cannes have a vast number of cinemas but, unless your French is good enough, you'll only be interested in the **Mercury** and the **Meliès** in Nice, which show undubbed foreign films. In summer, however, you should take advantage of the chance to see the stars on and off the screen, at the **Cinéma d'Eté** (Sporting Club, avenue Princesse Grace, in Monaco). This open-air cinema shows a different film each night, in English, with French sub-titles. Popular with the local celebrity residents such as Michael York. Bar as well.

Racing

For the hot summer nights, the chance to stay outside and gamble in the superb setting of the **Hippodrome de la Côte d'Azur** near the sea-front at Cagnes-sur-Mer. There are regular night-time races throughout the summer, plus two restaurants with views over the track.

CASINOS

The casinos of the *Côte d'Azur* are the temples of the good-life. Hopefully your luck at the tables will be such that you will be able to afford to visit them often!

The antics of the famed Italian Caltagirone brothers, who rolled in agony on the floor of the casino each time they lost, are frowned on these days. So be warned, gambling is a serious business. The cool, chic look is in: bejeweled women in elegant evening gowns and men wear tailored suits. In fact the really heavy gamblers win and lose their fortunes in the private rooms where the stakes can go up to 500,000 F.

Superstitions abound. In one English church, along the coast, only hymns above N° 36 are sung to stop the punters going off to place their bets on the heaven-sent numbers chosen by the vicar.

The King of local gambling legend is King Farouk of Egypt. At the Casino in Cannes, the foreign monarch was short of a King to complete the set for his winning hand, so he put himself in the game saying, "I am the fourth."

He got his money.

The superstitious should note that it is traditional in Monte-Carlo to touch the horse's knee of the statue in the lobby of the Hôtel de Paris for luck before going to the casino. It is not always effective. The practical should be aware that they must be over 21 and have a passport with them if they are going to try their hand against Lady Luck in any of the French casinos. When you win, don't forget to tip the staff with an ultra-casual *"Personnel, merci."* There is usually a slot at the table for that purpose.

CASINO DE MONTE CARLO

Place du Casino
MONTE CARLO
Tel: 93.30.99.31

The stuff of which legends are made. The elegant rococo interior has seen many fortunes won and lost. The man to try and imitate is Charles Wells who broke the bank here several times and in whose honor the song "I'm the man who robbed the bank in Monte Carlo" was written. But do keep in mind that was in 1891. The American room is an anachronistic mixture of slot machines and fine antiques. As it is very crowded during the peak summer months, you might as well spring for the entrance fee to the private salons, where the gambling is serious and the stakes high.

LOEWS CASINO

Avenue des Spélugues
MONTE CARLO
Tel: 93.50.65.00.

A Casino in the American style – big, bubbly and relaxed, although

the dark decor does little to raise the spirits of players.

CASINO DE BEAULIEU

8, avenue Blumdell Mapple
BEAULIEU
Tel: 93.01.00.39.

Sedate and seductive, probably the most elegant of the casinos along the coast. There are no slot machines chattering away like an electronic menagerie to break the spell. If you want to take a break from the roulette table, there is an excellent restaurant as well.

CASINO DU SOLEIL

Avenue Félix Faure
MENTON
Tel: 93.57.11.31

Close to the border and a favorite with the smart Italian set. A spot for the quiet gambler. Restaurant.

CASINO DE LA SIESTA

Route du Bord de Mer
VILLENEUVE LOUBET
Tel: 93.33.31.31

For the trendy gambler. Part of a complex with seven discos, set beside the sea, it is for people who like to have all their pleasures at once.

CASINO DE JUAN-LES-PINS

Boulevard Paudoin
JUAN-LES-PINS
Tel: 93.61.01.29

A little off the jet-set track yet the elegant palm-fronted Casino is still a favourite with happy holiday.

CASINO MUNICIPAL DE CANNES

Palais des Festivals
La Croisette
CANNES
Tel: 93.38.12.11

In the *Bunker* (as locals describe the unprepossessing *Palais des Festivals* in Cannes), the Casino is nevertheless conveniently central.

PALM BEACH

Avenue Franklin Roosevelt
CANNES
Tel: 93.43.91.12

With Cannes as the home of petro-dollar wealth on the *Côte d'Azur*, here's your chance to see the rich on their home turf.

LOEWS CASINO LA NAPOULE

LA NAPOULE
Tel: 93.49.90.00

A touch of feminine charm has been added by taking advantage of recent changes in the French law to introduce women *croupiers*.

NIGHTCLUBS AND DISCOS

Curiously, all the sun-worshippers, who have spent the day working hard on their tan, like to spend the evening in dark crowded discos. But after hours of lounging on the beaches, it is good to have some exercise. Like all things in France, it is best if spiced with a heavy dose of romance, which is highly possible as the dance floor is usually a terrific pick-up spot.

To help overcome any language barriers, the Riviera smart-set have their own gadget to flash out their messages of love. The American-made Winkie, has become the seducer's latest weapon. It is a small badge with two flashing lights, one green, one red — Yes and No respectively.

Quite clear, unless of course you are colour-blind or — like many a continental disco-smoothy — wearing dark glasses.

The problem remains that the best discos, like the **Camargue** in Nice and **Les Caves du Roi** in Saint-Tropez, are the most difficult to get into. Dedicated to the beautiful people, it often means the wealthiest as well. But if you're not beautiful or rich your best bet — particularly in very fashion conscious Saint-Tropez — is best to be outrageous. If this still doesn't get you through the door, take comfort from the fact that the doorman of one exclusive club prides himself on having refused entry to a prince.

MONACO

JIMMY'Z DE LA MER

Monte Carlo Sporting Club
Avenue Princesse Grace
Tel: 93.30.71.71

JIMMY'Z

Place du Casino
Tel: 93.50.80.80

In the winter, **Jimmy'z** is near the Casino. In the summer, Regine's justly famous club moves to a superbly romantic setting at the **Sporting Club**. It is the home of the fabled jet-set. There you can see princesses in a twirl, playboys a-playing and elegant beauties. It is the stuff of which dreams are made. But be warned; it is expensive and impossible to get in if not well-dressed. After a certain hour, the young pretenders to the fortunes dancing away in Jimmy'z head for the **Parady'z.**

PARADY'Z
Sporting d'Eté
Avenue Princesse Grace
Tel: 93.30.71.71

The music is more upbeat and the open-air dance-floor is packed with the young *beau monde* of Monaco. The **Sporting** also houses the **Salle des Etoiles,** an immense space with its impressive roll-back roof, for cabarets and sumptious gala events.

NOROC
7, rue Portier
Tel: 93.25.09.25

Pretender to Régine's throne as Queen of the Nightclubs, is Mariana Simionescu, ex-wife of tennis star Björn Borg, who has opened her own disco and piano-bar. Something of a celebrity in her own right, her club attracts others, notably Prince Albert, and despite its sombre black and silver decor, it is rapidly becoming a *must* on the Monaco social scene.

THE LIVING ROOM
7, avenue des Spélugues
Tel: 93.50.80.41

A fashionable, discreet piano bar/ discotheque for the older crowd, and a popular late-night (or rather early morning) stop.

TIFFANY'S
3, avenue des Spélugues
Tel: 93.50.53.13

Popular with Princess Stephanie, it attracts the younger crowd – many of whom have tried and failed to get into the other, more formal, clubs. The **Tif**, as it's known, has the best music in Monte Carlo, and also has videogames at the bar.

NICE

LA CAMARGUE
Cours Saleya
Tel: 93.85.74.10

For the risk-takers, owner Roger Dalmas has dedicated his private club to the beautiful people only. The fun of the evening is knowing whether you qualify. It is worth the struggle to get in. The decor may be very *Homes and Gardens* but it has a sophisticated charm unmatched in Nice.

LE GRAND ESCURIAL
29, rue Alphonse Karr
Tel: 93.87.76.76

A converted cinema with Roman frescoes on the wall and an up-to-date light show with 6,000 flashing lights and lasers. Good mix of students, vacationers and business people.

FINDLATTERS
6, rue Lépante
Tel: 93.85 09.54

Your chance to meet a Swedish *au pair* or two (Scandinavians always go for the hot places). It has an exotic look and the best new-wave music in town. There's also a videobar and a late-serving restaurant.

THE BLUE SEA

26, quai Lunel
(on the old port of Nice)
Tel: 93.55.23.43

One of the "in" places for youngsters in Nice, with a trans-atlantic slant. The disco is called **New York** and the disc-jockey presides behind a bright yellow Oldsmobile. Next-door, the piano-bar has Brazilian music and views of Rio from the cabin of a Boeing 747.

CHEZ LES ECOSSAIS

6, rue Halevy
Tel: 93.87.92.00

Lots of slow dances in this British pub-style club for the older singles. (30/40). Jackets are mandatory for men.

THE BLUE BOY

9, rue Spinetta
Tel: 93.88.67.22

The crowd are all of different ages, classes, and colour but only one sex – male. A friendly club, but no ladies allowed.

ANTIBES AREA

LA SIESTA

Route du Bord de Mer
Between Antibes and
Villeneuve Loubet
Tel: 93.20.94.54

A must for the summer. You can boogey away in the open-air, beside the palm-fringed shore of the Mediterranean, on a dance-floor lit by burning torches. With seven dance floors, there is plenty of room for all the bronzed beach beauties. Casino.

LE FORT CARRE

Avenue du 11 Novembre
ANTIBES
Tel: 93.33.97.12

The old fortress of Antibes is the setting for this big disco for youngsters. Admission and drinks suitably modest.

ROLLER DISCO

35, route de Grasse
ANTIBES
Tel: 93.33.23.95

More to try as a novelty. A cold concrete barn of a place, but the one spot on the coast where you can roller skate and dance at the same time.

L'ERREUR

Route Nationale 7
VILLENEUVE-LOUBET
Tel: 93.20.94.54

The main error seems to be its out-of-the-way situation, squashed between the railway line and Marina Baie des Anges. Good piano bar, with disco beside it and a *recherché* line in music.

CLUB 4
4, place du Château
HAUT-DE-CAGNES
Tel: 93.73.16.94

A quaint vaulted cellar club, close to the magnificent château of this picturesque hill-village. Plenty of atmosphere – but small.

CANNES

LE STUDIO CIRCUS
48, boulevard de la Republique
Tel: 93.38.32.98

Where petro-dollar wealth mixes with Mediterranean chic. The *in* place in Cannes where most people are kept out. At festival time it plays host to a parade of showbiz stars. Relatively new, very big and extremely loud.

THE WHISKY A GOGO
115, avenue des Lérins
Tel: 93.38.20.63

Spacious disco with good music, laser light-shows and video projections. Well-known by locals and tourists alike. Open all the year round.

CLUB 06
5, rue des Belges
Tel: 93.68.00.33

The decor is a bit musty, but you can watch yourself dancing on the video screen. There is an all night pizza-parlour to satisfy the hunger pangs.

LE JANE'S
Hôtel du Gray d'Albion
38, rue des Serbes
Tel: 93.48.54.54

Piano-bar and disco at very moderate prices, in addition to a restaurant that certainly holds it own. Small dance floor.

GALAXY CLUB
Palais des Congrès
La Croisette
Tel: 93.38.12.11

On the third floor of the Palais des Congrès, the Galaxy has a clear image of its customers. No jeans are allowed and the men must wear a jacket. The decor is subdued, the welcome a bit frosty.

PLAYGIRL
88-90, avenue de Lérins
Tel: 93.43.11.40

Something of a trip back in time. A big dance hall with baroque decor, plenty of fountains and Greek busts.

SAINT-TROPEZ

LES CAVES DU ROY
Hôtel Byblos
Avenue Paul Signac
Tel: 94.97.00.04

Not easy to get into! Possibly the most fashionable of all the discotheques in the South of France, where stardom is often out-rivalled by outrageousness. From June to mid-September.

L'APHRODISIAQUE
35, rue du Général-Allard
Tel: 94.97.01.15

Discotheque and private club, where you can dance away till dawn. For the young, bronzed and famous.

LE PAPAGAYO
Quai de l'Epi
Tel: 94.97.07.56

More for the camping-car society than the jet-set. But great view of the port from the terrace, and very up-beat music.

L'ESQUINADE
Rue du Four
Tel: 94.97.38.09

Very difficult to get into. But the service is fantastic and the music right up to the moment. One of the stopping-off places for the millionaires doing the Saint-Tropez circuit.

LE PIGEONNIER
11, rue de la Ponche
Tel: 94.97.36.85

Birds of a different feather flock together. Mainly, but not exclusively, a gay club known for its frivolous fun.

BARS, PIANO-BARS AND CAFES

MONACO

BAR OF THE HOTEL DE PARIS
Place du Casino
Tel: 93.50.80.80

Obligatory pilgrimage for all those who want to see the latest in high fashion, compare jewels or simply listen to society gossip. Good place to lap up that specific Monaco ambiance, where the scent is wealth and the name of the game is to flaunt it.

BAR OF THE HOTEL HERMITAGE
Square Beaumarchais
Tel: 93.50.67.31

A superb view over the port and the Palace. The old town beyond make this one of the most pleasant bars in Monaco to take an *apéritif*. You might also catch a glimpse of the odd star like Charlton Heston, Mel

Brooks or Prince, who have all sampled the Hermitage's *Belle Epoque* charm.

CAFE DE PARIS
Place du Casino
Tel: 93.50.57.75

Bustling atmosphere, pleasant terrace where one can watch the world and all the beautiful people, go by. Brasserie-style restaurant, all the international newspapers – to the music of the inevitable slot machines. The bar is an excellent pick-up place.

FLASHMAN'S
7, avenue Princesse Alice
Tel: 93 30.09.03

For the nostalgic English (and others) looking for a good pint of beer and a relaxed pub atmosphere. The restaurant is homely, with good quality food.

LOBBY LOUNGE
Loews Hotel
Avenue des Spélugues
Tel: 93.50.65.00

The place to meet your friendly American conference-goer. Comfortable, relaxed piano-bar.

VILLEFRANCHE-SUR-MER

LES PALMIERS
Port of Villefranche-sur-Mer

Opposite the little chapel decorated by Jean Cocteau. English pub-style atmosphere.

NICE

BAR OF THE HOTEL NEGRESCO
Promenade des Anglais
Tel: 93.88.39.51

Worth a visit just to take a peek at the **Negresco** and its fabulous decor. It has probably the most kitsch toilets in the world – the Gents is fashioned after a Crimean war bunker. Quiet, civilised bar with good service.

LES PONCHETTES
Cours Saleya
Vieux Nice
Tel: 93. 80.42.40

The trendy bar of Nice – the place to see the latest look. Big terrace, full in summer.

LE VALENTINO
3, Promenade des Anglais
Tel: 93.87.09.27

Moody black lacquer and gold piano-bar/restaurant. Good cocktails and friendly service – if a bit slow.

PAM PAM
Place Masséna
Tel: 93.80.21.60

Exotic, noisy cocktail bar, with a South American feel much loved by the young *Niçois*. The band sometimes gets carried away with the decibels but the elaborate cocktails will help deaden the pain, as well the pretty local girls.

LE CHARLOT
8, rue St François-de-Paule
Tel: 93.62.29.42

The "in" gay bar in Nice. Frivolous, friendly and usually full. Drinks reasonably priced.

LE FLORE
Place Magenta
Tel: 93.87.88.46

In the heart of Nice, a pavement terrace popular with the local Romeos, who eye the passing talent. Restaurant as well.

LE CRYSTAL
2, place Magenta
(Pedestrian Zone)
Tel: 93.87.85.30

Neighbour to Le Flore, it attracts lots of tourists during the summer content to while away the hours watching the world pass by. Superb ice-creams.

CLUB NAUTIQUE
50, boulevard Franck Pilatte
Tel: 93.89.32.97

Cocktails in a nautical setting with fine views of the sea and port.

JUAN-LES-PINS

PAM-PAM
137, boulevard Wilson
Tel: 93.61.11.05

A screeching parrot, Brazilian music and exotic cocktails have proved an infallible combination. This is where it all happens, even on the pavement at the height of the season.

CANNES

BAR OF THE HOTEL CARLTON
La Croisette
Tel: 93.68.91.68

A must at festival time if you like star-gazing. On the delightful terrace you can eavesdrop on the likes of Tony Curtis, Catherine Deneuve or Roger Moore, but you pay for the privilege.

BAR OF THE HOTEL MAJESTIC
La Croisette
Tel: 93.68.91.00

Another festival hot-spot equally popular during the summer, because of its sumptious terrace beside the swimming pool.

LE FESTIVAL
52, La Croisette
Tel: 93.38.04.81

Very popular with the cinema crowd for its vantage-point terrace, enormous sundaes – and good food.

LE BLUE BAR

La Croisette
Tel: 93.39.03.04

Close to the old Festival Hall. Another good look-out point for those wanting to study the beautiful people at leisure.

LE CINTRA

Place Charles de Gaulle
Tel: 93.39.13.43

A pleasant terrace that has become a hang-out for the bronzed youngsters of Cannes, particularly of the see-and-be-seen brigade.

LE RAGTIME

La Croisette
Tel: 93.48.47.10

Good situation – directly opposite the *Palais des Festivals*. Popular with the Cannois and jazz-lovers, it has a video system so that no matter where you sit you can see the piano-player. Restaurant as well.

LE ZANZY BAR

85, rue Félix Faure
Tel: 93.39.30.75

Something of a gay instution in Cannes, even attracting some of the big gay stars at festival time.

MOUGINS

L'ABREUVOIR DE MOUGINS

Mougins Village
Tel: 93.90.03.05

Slightly rustic atmosphere, but paradise for a Scotsman, with more than 100 different types of whiskey. Video music screen as well.

SAINT-TROPEZ

SENEQUIER

Quai Jean Juarès
Tel: 94.97.00.90

LE GORILLE

Quai Suffren
Tel: 94.97.03.93

Directly on the port and seemingly reserved for the bronzed and beautifuL, these are Saint-Tropez's traditional vantage points for seeing and being seen. Captures the whole essence of *Saint-Trop* – very pleasant off-season but impossibly crowded in July/August.

NANO

Place de l'Hôtel-de-Ville
Tel: 94.97.01.66

Young and trendy, even gay atmosphere in this popular bar-restaurant, open all year round.

LE BISTROT DES LICES

3, place des Lices
Tel: 94.97.29.00

NIGHTLIFE

Popular piano-bar that serves as a good rendez-vous before attacking the disco's.

LE CAFE DES ARTS
Place des Lices
Tel: 94.97.02.25

Another *in* place, but away from the madding crowds on the port. Enjoy the traditional *pastis* in what used to be an authentic village café on the *place des boules* and which still has a definite shabby charm.

Roger Laing

ROGER LAING is an international journalist, who covers the Riviera for several major English-language newspapers. He lives in Nice and spends his nights in assorted Riviera hot spots.

9
THE SPORTING LIFE

204 | You Are What You Play
206 | Helpful Numbers
212 | The Verdon: A New Sports Area

How much discrimination is there on the Riviera if you show up at the beach without a suntan and fifteen pounds overweight in the middle of summer? Don't try to find out. Although the Riviera is not quite as beauty or health conscious as southern California, being white and fat is definitely OUT between May and October. It is only slightly less OUT during the winter when you can get by with a mere facial tan from skiing.

This might seem unfair, but it's difficult not to be tan and healthy in the South of France because so much of Riviera life is spent outdoors. Locals and visitors mix and meet on the beaches and ski-slopes, where the social life is more active and inventive than in the discos or the bars.

At the same time, the people living in the south are not sports fiends. They don't bore you with recitations about how far they have jogged or what's new in weight-lifting equipment. But it is rare to find someone who is not interested in one sport or another. The opportunity for exercise is so vast that it's hard to pass up.

The first time I interviewed Jacques Médecin, the mayor of Nice who is always tan, most of our conversation was about fly-fishing and golf. When I first talked to Jacques Lebraty who runs the CERAM graduate school of business at Sophia Antipolis, the discussion immediately turned to tennis. Marc Journoud at Dow Chemical prefers to discuss his company's activities on one of the many golf courses in the area.

Printer Alain Rouland goes water-skiing at Golfe-Juan in the morning and at lunch, and my dentist takes his windsurfer out between appointments. Almost every woman I know has her own ranking of gym, dance and aerobic classes (Princess Caroline likes the gym at Loews' Hotel in Monaco) based on personal investigations of the hundreds available.

You Are What You Play

Skiing in April at the small resort of Gréolières, a bare hour's drive from the coast, you can look down from the top of the mountain to see spring on the hills and summer at the beach. You can do almost anything, almost all year round.

It is difficult to choose what to do because there is so much to choose from. My banker plays tennis three times a week, skis on weekends in winter, goes up to Gourdon for hang-gliding during the spring, windsurfs after work in the summer and likes to ride horseback in the Var. Somehow, he still has time to jog.

Everything is rentable and the competition among commercial outlets is hot enough to make prices fairly reasonable and equipment easy to find. People are also laid back and friendly when it comes to athletics. You can talk yourself into a pool for a workout with a water polo team, get into conversation with fellow windsurfers, or pick up a casual tennis game without suffering from over-earnestness or country club snobbery. Golf is played in jeans, it seems almost illegal to play tennis in whites and most hotels have pools and access to the beach and tennis courts. The Riviera also caters to kids. Most pools have children's areas, some ski resorts have babysitters-on-skis to take care of your offspring, and they can get lessons in practically any sport imaginable.

There are numerous organized competitive events throughout the year — triathlons, marathons, swimathons, windsurfathons and professional and amateur golf and tennis tournaments. The easiest way to keep in touch is to read **Nice-Matin**, which dedicates more space to sports than any other topic.

Of course, you don't need to over-exert. The regional sport is *pétanque* or *boules*, a very restful way to while away summer afternoons. The champions are all from the shores of the Med, but anyone can play, and every year **Nice-Matin** features a big color picture of Yves Montand playing in Saint-Paul-de-Vence. There are also fine marked hiking trails and numerous camping sites throughout the back country. You can follow well-marked trails that criss-cross the mountains and countryside, including the very descriptive *Balcon de la Côte d'Azur*. Then there's the whole spectrum of indoor sports. There are hundreds of dojos around for judo, karate, aikido and other martial arts. Squash, bowling and weight-lifting can also be performed out of the sun.

The Mediterranean is itself a center for sports. Although cleaner in some parts than others, it is still a wonderful area for diving, swimming (especially from the rocky Esterel between La Napoule and Saint Raphael), windsurfing (the winds in the summer are often gentle, and suitable for beginners), sailing and water-skiing. There are numerous marinas where you can rent or buy boats, and one relaxing sport is simply walking through the marinas to look at other people's boats.

If you get tired of all this strenuous activity, you can sit on a beach. Boy and girl-watching is also a big sport and a lot of people exercise their eyeballs at places with weird names like *Waikiki Plage.* However, it can cost you over fifty francs for a mattress at a private beach, not to mention the drinks and the dinner, so maybe a bit of simple strenuous exercise isn't such a bad idea after all.

HELPFUL NUMBERS

CENTRE INFORMATION JEUNESSE
Tel: 93.80.93.93

LA DIRECTION DEPARTEMENTALE TEMPS LIBRE, JEUNESSE ET SPORTS
Tel: 93.07.37.38

AVIATION

AERODROME INTERNATIONAL CANNES-MANDELIEU
269, Avenue Francis Tonner, 06150
CANNES LA BOCCA.
Tel: 93.47.11.00

You can rent a plane with or without a pilot.

BICYCLING

Perhaps the greatest danger on French roads are the cyclists but every sports shop still sells the latest gear. Pedal as though you own the road. The automobilists will be annoyed but you'll hopefully avoid an accident.

COMITE DEPARTEMENTAL
c/o F. Parcillie, Le Jura A
12 boulevard Henri Sappia
06000 NICE
Tel: 93.51.22.56

BOULES

The Mediterranean version of bowling can be played virtually anywhere but every town has a number of "boulodromes" for the real fanatics. Anytime you see four or more of the locals standing together, there is probably a game of *boules* going on. This is the one sport taken seriously on the Riviera, so wait for an introduction before asking to join in.

CAMPING

CENTRE DEPARTEMENTAL DE CAMPING – INFORMATION

Office du Tourisme de
Nice-Parking, Parking Ferber
06200 NICE
Tel: 93.21.05.21

CAVING

There are thousands of caves hidden in nearby gorges,
hills and mountains.

COMITE DEPARTEMENTAL

130 boulevard de Cessole
06000 NICE
Tel: 93.81.42.15

DIVING

Many hotels, beaches and sports stores rent diving equipment. The best place to dive is along the Esterel.

COMITE DEPARTEMENTAL

FORT CARRE
06600 ANTIBES
Tel: 93.95.05.65

FISHING

You can rent boats at most marinas to go fishing in the Mediterranean but locals prefer going into the mountains to fish trout in the stream-like rivers. Get a permit or get arrested.

FEDERATION DEPARTEMENTALE DES SOCIETES DE PECHE

20 boulevard Victor Hugo
06000 NICE
Tel: 93.03.24.09

LA MAREE DES ILES

Quai des Pecheurs
Port de Plaisance
06310 BEAULIEU
Tel: 93.01.70.71

GOLF

The golf courses are open throughout the year and are somewhat congested during the summer. Depending on conditions, most of them permit guest players with green fees ranging from about 130 F during the week to 155 F on weekends (per person).

GOLF BASTIDE DU ROY
BIOT
Tel: 93.65.08.48
18 Holes

GOLF CLUB DE CANNES-MANDELIEU
MANDELIEU
Tel: 93.49.55.39
18 Holes

COUNTRY CLUB DE CANNES
MOUGINS
Tel: 93.75.79.13
18 Holes

MONTE CARLO GOLF CLUB
MONT AGEL-LA TURBIE
Tel: 93.41.09.11
18 Holes

GOLF DE VALBONNE
VALBONNE
Tel: 93.42.OO.08/05.29
18 Holes

GOLF DE VIEVOLA
TENDE
Tel: 93.04.61.02
9 holes

HANG-GLIDING

The winds are not always strong enough for windsurfing but the currents are great for hang- gliding. Favored locations are near Gourdon and Fayence.

ECOLE FRANCAISE DE VOL LIBRE
LA COLMIANE
Tel: 93.02.83.50

FEDERATION FRANCAISE VOL LIBRE
54bis, rue de la Buffa
06000 NICE
Tel: 93.88.62.89

HIKING AND MOUNTAINEERING

You can walk from Nice to Holland or from Menton to Spain on the national hiking paths known as *Les Grandes Randonées* (*GR*). Many bookstores sell maps for the *GR*'s (if in doubt, ask for the *Cartes I.G.N* – pronounced Eee-Jay-Enn) and there are a number of books detailing special walks around the Riviera.

ASSOCIATION DEPARTEMENTALE DES RELAIS ET ITINERAIRES (ADRI)
14 boulevard Victor Hugo
04000 DIGNE
Tel: 92.31.07.01

COMITE REGIONAL (FFM)
15 avenue Jean Medecin
06000 NICE
Tel: 93.87.95.41

COMITE DEPARTEMENTAL RANDONNEE PEDESTRE
2 rue Deloy,
06000 NICE
Tel: 93.31.76.64

SENTIERS AMITIES MONTAGNE
70 boulevard Perrier
06110 LE CANNET
Tel: 93.45.16.43

HORSEBACK RIDING

There are stables all over the place with riding costs averaging about 50 francs an hour. Like elsewhere in the world, the horses range from nags to nobles. You can even play polo.

COMITE REGIONAL D'EQUITATION DE RANDONNEE DES ALPES MARITIMES
Le Mas de La Jumenterie
route de St Cézaire
06460 ST VALLIER DE THIEY
Tel: 93.42.62.98

COMITE HIPPIQUE DEPARTEMENTAL
Stade Municipal des Sports
Parc Layet
06700 ST LAURENT DU VAR
Tel: 93.20.99.64

ASSOCIATION DE POLO DE CANNES MANDELIEU
Tel: 93.36.81.93

HUNTING

My neighbor keeps giving me fowl so I know they're out there. But the French are extremely fanatic when they take to the fields so be careful.They act like they are looking for criminals rather than shooting game.

FEDERATION DEPARTEMENTALE DES CHASSEURS
(ALPES- MARITIMES)
P.A.L.7 M.I.N. St Augustin
06042 NICE
Tel: 93.83.82.39

PARACHUTING

COMITE DEPARTEMENTAL
22 rue Assalit
06000 NICE
Tel: 93.85.18.54

ROWING

If you really are not ambitious you can rent pedal boats (about 40 F an hour) at most beaches but there is also some white water rafting and kayaking, on the Loup river, for example. Don't expect the Salmon River, however, especially in summer. The Grand Canyon du Verdon is more exciting.

LAC DE ST CASSIEN
Autoroute A8
LES ADRETS

Row boats and windsurfers are rentable on this freshwater lake just off the autoroute.

ASSOCIATION PLEIN AIR NATURE: ALPES DE HAUTE PROVENCE
Section Kayak
14 boulevard Victor Hugo
04000 DIGNE
Tel: 92.31.51.09

COMITE DEPARTEMENTAL
c/o P.SALENGH
51 chemin de la Campanette
Les Eucalyptus
06800 CAGNES SUR MER
Tel: 93.07.82.15

SAILING

Almost every town on the Mediterranean has a port with boats to rent or buy. The best way to find out the going prices is to drop into the yacht clubs or pubs. Most of the clubs also teach sailing.

LIGUE PROVENCE COTE D'AZUR
20 rue des Palmiers
06600 ANTIBES
Tel: 93.34.79.07

AQUASPORT
Port Gallice
06160 JUAN LES PINS
Tel: 93.61.20.01

CAMPER & NICHOLSONS YACHT SERVICES
Port Canto
06407 CANNES
Tel: 93.43.16.75

SOUTH OF FRANCE BOATING
Marina Baie des Anges
VILLENEUVE LOUBET
Tel: 93.20.55.16

YACHT CLUB D'ANTIBES
Ecole de Voile
Tel: 93.61.01.42

YACHT CLUB BEAULIEU/ SAINT JEAN
Quai White Church
Port de Plaisance
06310 BEAULIEU
Tel: 93.01.14.44

YACHT CLUB DE MONACO
Cale de Halage
quai Albert 1er
Tel: 93.30.63.63

SKIING

The two main slopes for Riviera skiers are **Isola 2000** and **Auron** (both about an hour and a half from Nice) but there are a number of smaller resorts. Day tickets cost 70-95 F, rental of skis boots and poles is about 80 F and there are buses to the slopes from the airport and train station in Nice. For people renting apartments, Isola 2000 has a great scheme. If there is no sun during a consecutive three- day period, you get a week free in the same type of apartment.

OFFICE DU TOURISME
06420 ISOLA 2000
Tel. 93.23.10.50.

OFFICE DU TOURISME
AURON
Tel: 93.23.02.66

CROSS-COUNTRY SKIING

LE COMITE REGIONAL COTE D'AZUR-CORSE DE LA FEDERATION FRANCAISE DE SKI
Commission de Fond
39, rue Pastorelli
06000 NICE
Tel: 93.80.65.77

SQUASH

Squash is picking up but growing a little more slowly than in other parts of the world because of the summer heat.

ANTIBES SQUASH CLUB
Tel: 93.33.53.33

NICE SQUASH CLUB VAUBAN
Avenue du Maréchal Vauban

Tel: 93.26.09.78

LOU PISTOU: ST-LAURENT-DU-VAR
Avenue du Zoo
Tel: 93.31.05.44

SWIMMING

One of the world's top long-distance female swimmers works out with the club in Antibes and every medium-sized community on the Riviera has a swimming-pool and team. The Masters program for older swimmers is much less advanced than in the United States, but you can join one club at:

CENTRE NAUTIQUE
Avenue Jules Grec
ANTIBES
Tel: 93.33.26.99

TENNIS

Almost everyone you meet on the Riviera has, or has access to, a tennis court. Most hotels also have their own courts or can get you onto a local court. You can visit a number of the clubs and usually pick up a game without too much trouble. Fees vary but are usually around 35/50 F an hour.

LIGUE COTE D'AZUR
5, avenue Suzanne Lenglen
06000 NICE
Tel: 93.53.92.98

SOPHIA COUNTRY CLUB
Biot-Sophia Antipolis
06560 VALBONNE
Tel: 93.65.26.65

The newest and brightest (there are no automobiles or autoroutes nearby) club on the Riviera, located in 31 acres of woodland with Yannick Noah's coach, Patrice Hagelauer, as director. Tennis holidays, junior tennis competition, private lessons, and training for players and coaches are available.

TENNIS ECOLE DE VILLENEUVE LOUBET
Route de Grasse
06270 VILLENEUVE LOUBET
Tel: 93.20.60.09
57 courts

WATER-SKIING & WINDSURFING

Windsurfers are rented at many sports shops and at almost every beach on the coast. Rental costs range from 35/50 F an hour and lessons go for between 75/90 F an hour. A six-minute session on water skis costs about 70 F.

Joel Stratte-McClure

JOEL STRATTE-McCLURE is a freelance journalist who has been living in the South of France for the last two years. He writes for numerous international publications and is the publisher of "Sophialet", a newsletter about the Sophia Antipolis high-technology park.

THE VERDON: A NEW SPORTS AREA

France's Grand Canyon is a superb narrow slash forged by the torrent of Verdon through crevices in the calcareous rock of Upper Provence's high plateaus. The vertical drop is breathtaking. The road around it, begun on the northern crests in the late twenties, was completed after World War II along the more spectacular southern side, an 80-kilometer drive called the *Corniche Sublime.* At the western end of the gorges is the small town of **AIGUINES** where the varnished tiles of a 17th-century castle glisten in the sun. Below is the incredibly blue lake created by the barrage of Sainte-Croix: 2500 acres of woodland and several villages were engulfed and the inhabitants moved to higher places like **LES SALLES**, where little ladies in black still peer through the waters looking for a trace of their old homes. Europe's largest artificial lake has opened up a whole new sports area: rollicking winds for windsurfers, waters well-stocked with fish, a public lake-shore with campsites and many beaches. Villages like **BAUDUEN** that once were high and dry are trying to become appropriately nautical. You can stay here at **l'Auberge du Lac** (Tel: 94.70.08.04). Open from March 28 to Nov 11, it has 10 rooms from 180-220 F.

The road along the northern side of the Verdon Canyon can be reached with a short detour to **MOUSTIERS-SAINTE-MARIE**, dominated by two cliffs strangely chained together with a star by a returning crusader and known for its *faience* pottery, with amusing *grotesque* flower or bird designs. Before deciding what to buy, enjoy eating off typical Moustiers plates in **Les Santons** on the Place de l'Eglise, Tel: 92.74.66.48 (phone ahead during the high season). Meals 124-185 F.

LE GRAND CANYON DU VERDON

For strenuous hikers, a tough six hour trek along the canyon can be followed along a red and white marked *sentier de grande randonnee* (GR4) between the Chalet de la Maline and the Point Sublime. In season (but not the rest of the year), taxis are available for the return trip. Plan carefully with area maps of the Grand Canyon.

A novel but less strenuous hike follows the old road built by the Romans. Follow in the steps of pilgrims, monks and knight-crusaders who trekked during the Middle Ages from Moissac-Bellevue towards Draguignan or vice- versa, passing on the way the ruins of **Florielle**, a Cistercian abbey older than the Thoronet, and the Grimaldi Tower at **Tourtour.**

For horse-riding enthusiasts, at 6 km from Draguignan, the

SPORT

Relais de Montéou on the Route de Grasse (Tel: 94.68.30.24) has info as the central committee of the *Equitation de Randonnees du Var.*

There are also kayak facilities for the intrepid along the torrents of the Verdon.

Mavis Guinard

MAVIS GUINARD, an American journalist and translator, divides her time between Switzerland and the South of France. Her features on both areas have appeared in the "International Herald Tribune".

10
BRINGING THE KIDS ALONG TOO

219	Where to Stay
220	Eating Out with Your Kids
222	Interesting Things for Kids to Do
223	Time Out
224	For the Energetic
226	The Beaches and the Sea
227	Walks and Outings with Children

Think of all the Hollywood movies you've seen about the Riviera. How many kids have even a walk-on part? Not many. The French Riviera is not associated with children. They are not allowed in casinos; they are noticeably absent in elegant restaurants; and you can't get many of them into an open sports car. They see no interest in shopping for designer clothes, looking at impressionist paintings, or tasting local wines. They get carsick, hungry, sunburnt and tired. They fidget at concerts, knock over vases in shops, and run riot in cafés.

However, despite the obvious good sense of heading for the Riviera *à deux* , and leaving the kids in the capable hands of your old-fashioned English nanny (as Clark Gable would have done), thousands of you will arrive every year with children in tow, your luggage bulging with stuffed animals and with assorted inflatable equipment for the beach. What kind of welcome can you expect? Where should you go and what should you look for, to ensure a pleasant, trouble-free holiday?

The French Riviera can, in fact, be an excellent place to spend a holiday with children, if certain precautions are taken in advance. It is, after all, a Mediterranean country, where the foibles of the very young are looked on with indulgence. Though your little angels may spill your neighbours' drinks, or smear ice-cream on their Ferrari, they will usually be greeted with good-humour and tolerance. Very young children will get you preferential treatment in offices, shops and supermarkets. Women will stop in the street to comment and praise, but also to advise you on their upbringing. Total strangers will thrust unsuitable and sticky things into their hands, without request or provocation.

This welcome wears thinner at periods of the year where the *Côte d'Azur* is overwhelmed by the youth of Europe released from school and, apparently, from all other restraints. At such times, when the beach-attendants look as though they are reaching breaking-point, and you fear that your local restaurateur may empty the next plate of *bouillabaisse* over your offspring's head, it is wise to know where your children can go to let off steam.

There are, in fact, many wonderful places which are ideal for children, but hidden among the more adult attractions. This guide will tell you where to find them.

WHERE TO STAY

Many children find hotel quarters too cramped, so you may be looking for a house or apartment to rent. If you are extremely lucky, you will find a villa with a garden, or an apartment with a terrace at a reasonable price, but not in the high season (mid-June to mid- September), and only if you have friends on the spot who can look for one for you. Otherwise, you may decide to rent a camping-car or caravan. If so, avoid the campsites on the immediate coast, which are cramped and noisy, and go five or ten miles inland, where you will get a better welcome at lower rates, and where your children will have room to run around. Any tourist office will give you a copy of the *Guide des Campings et Caravanings des Alpes Maritimes* from the **CRT** (*Comité Régional du Tourisme*).

If you do stay in hotels, many of them are well-prepared to greet young guests. The pricing-policy of the hotel will give you some indication of the management's policy. **Loews** (La Napoule and Monte Carlo), for example, does not charge extra for children under 12 (see **Where to Stay** under the city concerned). The **Martinez** and the **Carlton** (both in Cannes) have a similar policy. Children over 12 are charged about 250 F a night, which is a considerable savings on the adult price, even if it's not cheap.

In lower-category hotels, the rates for children can be very reasonable. **Le Cagnard** (3*) in the Haut de Cagnes charges 120 F, and 30 F for breakfast. The **Astor** (2*) in Antibes only charges 60 F (they also rent little appartments with kitchens, which is nice for families). The **Hotel du Petit Louvre** (1*) in Nice adds 30% to the room-price if a child is added.

Smaller hotels are usually partial to children, because they sleep in the same room as their parents and pay extra. Very few hoteliers have hard and fast rules about how to charge, so feel free to negotiate an arrangement and a price which suits both you and the hotel.

EATING OUT WITH YOUR KIDS

Taking your kids to eat out is both much harder and much easier than in countries like Britain and America. It is harder because so few restaurants do anything special for children. High-chairs and children's menus are very rare, and dinner service often starts late in the evening. On the other hand, many restaurants are extraordinarily tolerant: even in the height of the summer, in a packed restaurant, with tourists queuing to get in, I have seen waiters pause to joke with children, or bring them extra goodies.

In the last five years, a number of fast-food eating-houses (serving food that is only edible by the under-16) have opened on the Riviera. You will find representatives of these chains in the major cities and tourist-centers — Nice (on avenue Jean Médecin and in the pedestrian area); Cannes (on rue d'Antibes) and Villeneuve-Loubet (near marina, Baie des Anges). Perhaps the best, for service and quality of food is **Quick** (a French chain), but all chains will provide the standard fare, tasteless and uniform enough to please your young ones.

Somewhat more varied, but also appreciated by the young are the *crêperies* (serving pancakes) and the *pizzerias*, where the atmosphere is usually relaxed, the service fast, and the clientele unconcerned by noise from adjoining tables. You will find innumerable *crêperies* and *pizzerias* in all the areas where tourists congregate (especially Juan-les-Pins, Cannes, and the pedestrian streets of Nice).

If your children are good in restaurants, branch out, and try them on more adventurous food. If you confide in your waiter, you can get your food served any way you want, with extra plates or little side-portions for children. Many restaurants won't charge for an extra dish if they know what's happening in advance.

If, on the other hand, your children are monsters at the

dining-table, here are a few addresses where even the worst behaviour will be greeted with a professional shrug.

LA MURENE

Boulevard de la Croisette

Beach restaurant near the Miramar Beach

CANNES

Tel: 93.94.20.88

Has a children's menu, and a more relaxed attitude to children than some of the snobbier Cannes beach-restaurants.

HIPPOPOTAMUS

16, avenue Félix Faure

NICE

Tel: 93.92.42.77

Good honest cuisine, in large quantities, and a children's menu for about 40 F.

MARINELAND RESTAURANT

Just off the RN7 road from Antibes to Cagnes-sur-Mer

BIOT

Tel: 93.33.49.49

After a couple of hours of dolphins and penguins, you may be glad to find that Marineland has a restaurant, and that the children's menu is only 39 F.

HOTEL RESTAURANT LES FLOTS

Rue des Iles
Just off the public beach
JUAN-LES-PINS

A good address if you're spending a day on the beach at Juan. Sophie and Gyl can fix anything from a sandwich to a full meal, to be eaten under the pines.

HOTEL GRIL CAMPANILE

On the RN7, by the Cannes/ Mandelieu airport.
CANNES LA BOCCA
Tel: 93.48.69.47

An address you might be glad to have if you're on the road looking for a place to stop and eat. Has a children's menu.

CAFETERIA CASINO

Boulevard d'Alsace
CANNES
Avenue Général de Gaulle
LE CANNET
Rue Nicolas Aussel
JUAN-LES-PINS
Bord de Mer
VILLENEUVE-LOUBET
Railway Station
Avenue Thiers
NICE

At all the biggest of the **Casino**

chain of supermarkets, you can find a cafeteria, which serves remarkably good food at very reasonable prices indeed. These cafeterias are very popular with shoppers, because of the variety of the food, the good organisation, and the relaxed atmosphere. The children's menu can be as little as 10 F, which is hard to beat. However, all the food is on display, so you'll be lucky to spend that little!

CAFETERIA FLUNCH
Entrance to the Autoroute
ANTIBES

Lingostière, on the road to Digne.
WEST NICE

Rue Halévy (near Meridien hotel)
CENTRAL NICE

Flunch cafeterias are very similar in style to Casino. They are often found in the same locations as the big **Carrefour** chain of supermarkets. The children's menu is around 12 F. In some Flunch restaurants, children are fed for free on Tuesday evenings, and on Saturdays before 12 o'clock.

INTERESTING THINGS FOR KIDS TO DO

The wonderful thing about the Riviera is that it combines the entertainment you can find in towns with the pleasures of the countryside and the open air. There are sports facilities and amusement centers of all kinds, as well as places to walk, climb, run or slide on. For little kids, there are carousels, amusement parks, circuses, puppet shows, and little trains to ride on. In the center of the cities, or in shaded corners under the pines, there are little playgrounds with jungle-gyms: these can make a welcome break from the beach, and a chance to mix with other kids.

For older children, there are shows and exhibitions, roller-skating, table-tennis, and a thousand other sports (see also the chapter on Sports in this guide). All up and down the coast you will see the word *Location* (meaning "To Rent") on all kinds of sports-equipment, and practically all leisure-centers offer special lessons for kids — including tennis, windsurfing, sailing and skiing.

Here is a little selection, but keep your eyes open for more. Every year, new shows and amusements open on the Riviera.

TIME OUT

FREJUS SAFARI ZOO

By the Fréjus exit from the Autoroute. Follow the signs.
Tel: 94.40.70.65
Open from 10 am to 5 pm. Adults: 35 F
Children (over 3): 18 F

The zoos of the Riviera aren't very big, but they all have a lot of character, and are well-suited to trips with children. This one has lots of open spaces, trees and grass. It's a very nice place to go with a picnic, but beware of lamas and emus, wandering freely around in search of a spare sandwich!

CAP FERRAT ZOO

Boulevard Général de Gaulle
CAP FERRAT
Tel: 93.01.31.56
Hours: 9:30 am to 6 pm
Adults: 26 F, Children: 16 F

Another pleasant little zoo, but much smaller, with more animals in cages. There are a number of special attractions for children, including an excellent monkey-show. After the zoo, you can take the children to see the light-house at the end of the Cap, or down on the rocks to fish for crabs.

MARINELAND

Biot, at the crossroads of the RN7.
Tel: 93.33.49.49
Opens at 11 am
Shows at 2:30, 4:30 and 6 pm Under 12 years old: 30 F

Over 12 years old: 50 F

Offers one of the very best aquatic shows in Europe, with dolphins, seals, killer whales and other marine creatures. For those used to American standards of showmanship, the premises seem a little cramped and unsophisticated, but the trainers make up for it in skill and subtlety.

OCEANOGRAPHIC MUSEUM AND AQUARIUM

Avenue Saint-Martin

On the Rock

MONACO

Tel: 93.30.15.14

Open: July & Aug: 9 am to 9 pm
June & Sept: 9 am to 7 pm Oct-May: 9:30 am to 7 pm

Over 16: 40 F

6-16 & students: 20 F

Even very young children can enjoy this museum full of strange marine objects and creatures. If your children are sensitive, beware of one rather terrifying room full of skeletons and bottled sea-serpents! The aquarium houses a unique collection of Mediterranean and tropical fish, most of them in breathtaking colours.

Other museums in **Monaco** that could be interesting for kids, depending on their taste, are:

THE MUSEUM OF NAPOLEONIC SOUVENIRS
Prince's Palace

Toy soldiers.

THE WAX MUSEUM OF THE PRINCES OF MONACO
Rue Basse – on the Rock

THE GALEA COLLECTION OF DOLLS
National Museum
Avenue Princesse Grace

AUTOMOBILE MUSEUM
On the Autoroute, between Cannes and Antibes.
Open: 10 am to 7 pm
Adults: 25 F
Children: 15 F

For the fanatic and the connoisseur, an impressive collection of 200 antique and veteran cars.

FOR THE ENERGETIC

ROLLER-SKATING

Summer traffic being what it is, skates may be the fastest way to get around. You can rent them on the sea-fronts of Cannes, Juan-les-Pins and Nice. The best track is surely the **Promenade des Anglais** in Nice: one of the longest skating-surfaces in the world!

Roller Disco
Route de Grasse, near the Autoroute.
Tel: 93.33.23.95

A huge disco-cum-rollerdrome. Fun for youngsters of all ages, and very noisy. There's a 10-pin bowling-alley downstairs, for those who like quieter sports.

WATER SKIING

You can find water-skiing at several of the bigger beach-facilities – around the Gulf of Saint-Tropez, at Saint Raphaël, in Cannes, Juan-les-Pins and on the sea-front of Nice.

At **Port Bijou** in Cannes (near the Palm Beach/Bijou Plage, at the pointed end of the Croisette), your kids can waterski under the watchful eye of Bernard Lignac, who speaks excellent English. It costs 100 F a trip, 200 F for a lesson, and is open every day from June to September. For an appointment, call 93.43.83.10 in the evening.

SWIMMING

The biggest pool facilities on the Riviera are at **Antibes** (Avenue Jules Grec, just off the RN7). There is a big outdoor and indoor pool, a diving-pool, and two pools for little kids. You can get snacks there, it has a lovely view of the old city, and is a nice place to spend an afternoon with the family. It's open to the public from the end of the morning till 6 pm or 8 pm at night (check the rather complicated opening-times at 93.33.26.99). Adults cost 7 F and children 4 F.

In Cannes, go to the **Complexe Sportif de Montfleury** (93.38.75.78), which also has tennis courts and a skating rink. It's a bit more expensive than Antibes, but much less crowded. If your kids are little, you may prefer something on a smaller scale, such as the pool at **Marina Baie des Anges** (the extraordinary apartment complex in the shape of curved pyramids, at Villeneuve-Loubet Plage). The pool is just as extraordinary – egg-shaped, with a little island in the middle and a very extensive shallow paddling-space for the very young. You can rent a mattress and umbrella for 55 F a day (kids under 7 are free!) and this price also lets you use the beach. The pool is used by the rich and bejewelled who inhabit the Marina, an exotic clientele who give this pool a very unusual atmosphere.

CYCLES, MOTORBIKES and SCOOTERS.

If you have teenage children, the way for them to mix, meet and get around is on a *deux roues* (two wheels). France has very lax laws about teenagers driving *mobylettes* or *motos* (from the age of 14, you can ride more or less anything), and young Riviera-ites learn to shoot red lights before they learn to shave. If this hasn't convinced you to keep your children off wheels, here are some addresses.

CHENU
Boulevard Dugommier
ANTIBES
Tel: 93.33.89.75

CANELUNI
36, boulevard Maréchal Leclerc
BEAULIEU
Tel: 93.01.04.51

CYCLES REMY
22, avenue des Hespérides
CANNES
Tel: 93.44.66

CANNES LOCATION RENT
5, rue Alleis
CANNES
Tel: 93.39.46.15

LOCATION 2 ROUES
33, boulevard Guillaumont
JUAN-LES-PINS
Tel: 93.61.63.24

ARNAUD
4, rue Grimaldi
NICE
Tel: 93.87.88.55

LOCA DEUX ROUES
29, rue Gounod
NICE
Tel: 93.87.20.07

MINIATURE GOLF

As you wander around the Riviera, you will find plenty of mini-golf courses: near Sainte-Maxime, near Marineland (Biot, Antibes), and in Monaco (Parc Princesse Antoinette). There are at least two in Menton, which is very suitable for such a sedate city, one at the Parc de la Madone, and the other (the **Mini-golf du Pian**) on the avenue Blasco Ibanez.

TENNIS

Very few tennis clubs don't have special programs or lessons for children, and the list would be too long for this guide. Our advice: drop by the nearest club, and if you are greeted with a smile and helpful information, sign on. Here are four clubs where our children were well-taught.

SOPHIA COUNTRY CLUB
Sophia Antipolis, Valbonne
Tel: 93.65.26.65

Offers weekend, 5-day or 7-day courses, starting July 1st.

TENNIS CANNES MARINA
Route du Golf
Mandelieu/La Napoule
Tel: 93.49.79.27

Intensive or semi-intensive courses.

TENNIS ECOLE DE VILLENEUVE-LOUBET
Route de Grasse Villeneuve-Loubet
Tel: 93.20.60.09

Tennis-school with 57 courts.

TENNIS MONTALEIGNE
between Saint-Laurent and La Gaude

Lessons cost 70 F for half-an-hour, and they offer four 2-hour courses, including video feedback, for 400 F.

THE BEACHES AND THE SEA

More than anyone, your children will take advantage of the round-the-clock summer action, along the beaches and sea-fronts. It's a living show where everyone can join in.

Real beach-lovers, lovers of endless sands, of dunes and rolling surf, will be a little disappointed by the Riviera, which are often covered in pebbles or rocks. You do, however, come for the bubbling life along the coast, which spills out onto these little beaches.

The sociable and gregarious will pick **Juan-les-Pins** and the most accessible beaches of **Saint-Tropez.** You may have to step over your neighbors to go for a swim, but everything is provided. Children in particular are offered endless delights: things to float on, ride on, drive in, chew on — all at varying levels of sophistication and cost.

The socially conscious, on the other hand, will go for the more exclusive, private beaches of **Cannes**, or the **Monte Carlo** beach, where their offspring can mix with those of the famous or, at least, those of the rich. They will avoid the stretch between **Saint-Aygulf** and **Fréjus**, or from **Antibes** to **Villeneuve Loubet**, invaded by campers and trippers (and correspondingly free of snobs).

The retiring, finally, will hunt for little beaches at **Cap d'Ail**, near Monaco, or on the Esterel, by **Théoule-sur-Mer**. They will clamber down from the road into little creeks and coves, which they will share with a select few, while their children dive and swim among the rocks.

(For detailed information, see **Beaches and the Sea** under each corresponding area)

EXCURSIONS: WALKS AND OUTINGS WITH CHILDREN

If your children are teenagers, you should head up into the mountains, where you will find an unlimited choice of hiking trails. Within a couple of hours of the coast, there are mountains of over 10,000 feet, there is the **Mercantour National Park** spread across the high Alpine passes, and the spectacular **Gorges du Verdon**. Trails are well-marked, hiking-maps are obtainable in most bookshops; ask for the *Cartes IGN* . You can also get all the advice and equipment you need in sports shops or the the major hiking-centers such as **St.Martin Vésubie** (North of Nice). The **Comité Régional du Tourisme** (55 Promenade des Anglais, 06300 Nice) will also provide you with a free brochure in English called "The Hiker's Handbook".

However, if your offspring are too young to tote a rucksack, or if your idea of a nice walk is a gentle stroll followed by a picnic, read on.

CAP D'ANTIBES

From the **Plage de la Garoupe**, you can walk for 5 or 600 yards along a paved path by the sea, with a very small public beach (rather rocky) at the end. A nice walk for toddlers. The Plage de la Garoupe itself has some nice paying beaches, with a big slide/raft for kids moored out in the bay. After the beach, drive up to the lighthouse (*Le Phare*), which you can visit, and admire the view.

THE SAINT-TROPEZ PENINSULA

Inland from **Saint-Tropez**, past **Cogolin** and along the N98, you will drive through many stretches of beautiful and unspoiled woodland. If the rush and bustle of the coast is getting too much for you, find a nice spot where your kids can trot around in the woods for a change.

THE ESTEREL

This is the red and rocky outcrop between **Saint-Raphaël** and **La Napoule**. The landscape is very wild, but there are many walks and places to picnic, with dramatic views over the sea.

ILE SAINTE MARGUERITE (ILES DE LERINS)

Take a boat from **Cannes** or **Juan-les-Pins**, and get away from it all. No vehicles are allowed on the island, and there are hundreds of little coves for picnics and swimming. (see **Cannes**).

FORET DE VALBONNE

A very beautiful little forest, now the site of the **Sophia Antipolis Science Park**, which is very well looked after (D35 and D103, just north of the Autoroute). There are wide paths, tracks for joggers and picnic areas. In July and August, many of the local inhabitants abandon the beaches to the tourists, and head for the peace and quiet of the woods. Twenty minutes from the **Forêt de Valbonne**, and less than fifty yards from the sea, there is also the **Parc Vaugrenier** (RN7 between Antibes and Villeneuve Loubet), which has wide grassy lawns as well as a forest, and is rather more crowded.

THE BAOU DE SAINT JEANNET

Saint Jeannet is a little village a few kilometers from **Vence**, easily accessible from **Cagnes-sur-Mer** or **Nice**, and a popular center for climbing or hiking. The trail up to the top of the **Baou** (the big rock that looms over the village) takes about an hour (one way), and can be handled by kids of 6 or over. There are lots of nice places to stop, and the view from the top is incredible.

CAP FERRAT

Cap Ferrat is the headland sticking out into the sea between **Villefranche** and **Beaulieu**. A path goes all round the point of the Cap, following the sea, and you get onto it, from the west side, at the **Plage Passable**, or from the east side at **Saint Jean-Cap-Ferrat**. This is one of the most beautiful walks of the Riviera, but avoid weekends in summer, when the path is crowded with Sunday walkers.

Brandy Kail

BRANDY KAIL is a writer and teacher, living and working on the Riviera, where she is bringing up her family of three children.

11
DOING BUSINESS ON THE RIVIERA

232 | Services and Science in the Sun
235 | The Tough Life
236 | Business Dining
237 | Business Contacts
238 | Banks
239 | Brokers
239 | Consulates
239 | Conventions and Conferences
240 | Lawyers
240 | Real-Estate Agencies
241 | Services

The first thing local or foreign businessmen living on the Riviera let visitors know is just how NICE it is to live down here. They delightfully recite the professional and personal conveniences of the area and you immediately wonder why you commute in New York or London, contend with the traffic problems in Los Angeles or live with lousy weather in Paris, Stockholm or Moscow.

The Riviera is a good place to work because most professionals (artists, bankers, brokers and lawyers) have chosen, and often claim to have made professional sacrifices, to live down here. Very few people are here against their will which makes it a productive, and fun, place to work.

Yves Crepet of **Dow Chemical France**, whose headquarters are in **Sophia Antipolis** (the booming 10,000 acre technology park located off the autoroute between Nice and Cannes), is a good example. From his office, you look out on the Alps beyond the corporate swimming-pool and tennis courts (which employees theoretically use only during lunch and before and after work). Crepet doesn't say anything — he just smiles.

I was so taken in by the good life I saw on the Riviera during a decade's worth of visits to the Cannes Film Festival, Monaco and Sophia Antipolis that I finally left Paris and moved down here.

Is life really this easy? Can people make money living in this type of environment? Yup!

Services and Science in the Sun

Jacques Médecin, the mayor of Nice and necessary contact for almost any significant business dealings on the Riviera, makes it clear that what you see is what you get.

The Riviera, contends Médecin, has become the frontier of new business. Income from science, services and light industry now rivals the $1 billion annual revenue from tourism that has been the area's traditional economic mainstay.

During the past twenty years, Médecin and his political cohorts made a concerted political decision to diversify from tourism and attract educational institutions, scientific ventures and high-tech industry. They encouraged the construction of new industrial zones, helped create the financial structure to attract large and small companies and gave a special boost to science and education.

Today there is a pleasant blend of Mediterranean climate and lifestyle with state-of-the-art technology, progressive business attitudes and a well-established communication, educational and scientific infrastructure.

"We are as capitalistic as ever and welcome foreigners who come work here or stay and start a business," Médecin has told me often.

After I moved south, Medecin gave speeches telling audiences I fell for the propaganda I wrote about the Riviera. In fact, it's true. The airport is a twenty minute drive from my house (where I am connected to the world via computers and modems) and there are direct flights to Paris, New York, London, Geneva and many other cities.

There is a great mix of French and international business people (**Merrill Lynch**'s 27 employees represent 12 different nationalities) in a wide variety of industries ranging from perfume (which still accounts for over 25 percent of all exports from the Riviera) to fashion (among them are Chacok and Jitrois) to multinationals like **Air France**, **IBM**, **Digital Equipment Corp.**, **Texas Instruments**, **Wellcome** and numerous others.

The Riviera's service sector, employing two-thirds of the population, has kept up with the economic growth. For example, the area has a banking network employing almost 6,000 persons at over 440 branches. Many French and international banks readily assist foreign firms in adapting to the local environment by quickly putting management in contact with local officials and business partners.

And once you're here, for business or pleasure, there are surprises around every corner. Telephone density is among the highest in France, the number of hospital beds per inhabitant is well above the norm and there are excellent educational facilities, including American, Anglo-American and international schools.

There is also competition between the different cities, towns, technology parks and industrial sites to attract new industry. Municipal and local agencies will sell you on the investment potential of the Riviera for your company though they admit that there are not the government subsidies you will find in Ireland or other parts of France. The quality of life, rather than financial incentives, is the main selling point.

Digital Equipment Corp. (**DEC**) moved to the Riviera primarily because "it made sense economically," says Michele Bonessa, DEC's manager of technical support services in Europe. There's an international atmosphere, excellent communications, good transport facilities and a pleasant environment.

Coopers & Lybrand recently came up with a dozen financial reasons to invest in the Riviera. They include up to 230 available types of grants, tax benefits and premiums; large concentration of French and international banking institutions; taxation on a cost-plus basis granted to corporate headquarters; lower local rates than in other parts of France; up to a three million franc tax-credit for research and development, and free remittance of funds originating from income and original investments for non-French residents.

For these and other reasons, American and British firms are scattered in different towns along the Mediterranean and contend there is little strain adapting to the environment. **Merrill Lynch** and **Citicorp** are located in Monaco, **Coopers & Lybrand** is represented by an associate firm in Nice and **Computerland** is in Saint Laurent du Var. **NCR**, **Rank Xerox**, **Wang** and other high-tech leaders have sales offices in the region, while **Sperry**'s international management center is in Saint Paul-de-Vence. Sophia Antipolis is already home to numerous international advanced technology companies, service and engineering firms, educational and training centers, research laboratories and light production facilities. Monaco, due to its relaxed tax laws, is the center of most financial activity.

Companies also flock to the area for conferences and conventions. The **Acropolis**, the Nice arts and convention center actively competes with the *Palais des Festivals* in Cannes, which hosts the

Cannes Film Festival, for international conferences. But even smaller communities — like Monaco, Menton, Grasse, Beaulieu, Sophia Antipolis and Antibes — also have their own conference facilities and visitors are accommodated in a number of hotels (there are 1,680 hotels on the Riviera) at varying prices.

The Tough Life

The pace is the pleasure, of course. There are few long business lunches here compared to Paris, and you are more likely to conduct negotiations during a round of golf, a sail on the Med or a run on the ski slopes rather than at a restaurant (though there is no shortage of good business lunch and dinner spots).

Things are relaxed. Few people wear ties and those that do take them take them off between May and September and work in shirtsleeves. There is rarely pressure to respect strict arrival and departure times at work, and many choose to work unusual hours for personal reasons.

Yet don't confuse the Riviera with Athens or Sydney. Things and people work! Most people (except for plumbers and electricians) are punctual, respect deadlines and even pay their bills — though usually under the table. Cash is preferred for most services to avoid the value-added-tax and higher than necessary income-tax declarations. In fact, it's rare to find the tradesmen who prefers a check.

Naturally this environment, which has attracted a number of inordinately wealthy inhabitants, has its share of sharks. Some them are selling a load of questionable investment opportunities. Watch out. The sun has gotten to a lot of them and the casinos may be as good a bet as some of their ploys.

However, if you've got venture capital, there are a number of worthwhile young start-up companies looking for funding. Entrepreneurs flock to southern France because of the large affluent market, talented labor pool and available financing.

Real estate has cooled off from the boom years of the 60's and 70's (though in Monaco and coastal areas, the limitation of land

sempé

keeps prices up), but there have recently been signs of a cautious revival of interest. Like elsewhere in the world, most Riviera investors have found it more profitable to play the financial markets during the past three years than put their money in tangibles. But there is no shortage of real estate agents who will tell you now is the time to buy.

The best way to make business contacts, besides through friends, is to attend a lunch with one of the international service organizations. **Rotary International**, **Lions International** and other organizations are flourishing on the Riviera and welcome visitors from the United States and other countries. Their meetings are listed in **Nice-Matin**.

There's no question that the Riviera will keep moving in a business-oriented direction. The **Nice-Cote d'Azur International Airport** is being expanded, the new **Arenas Business Center**, which will face the airport, is billed as "off the plane into the office". **Arenas** will feature office locations, hotel rooms and a shopping and sports center when it opens 1987. It probably should be advertised as "off the plane, into the pool -- and then into the office."

BUSINESS DINING

I do not like any of the Michelin three star restaurants on the Riviera and generally prefer taking business acquaintances to the following (somewhat-sophisticated) eateries — or barbequing in my back yard. I also tend to go for the *menu de dégustation* which provides first-timers with a light touch of the house specialities.

CANNES

LA PALME D'OR

73, boulevard de la Croisette.
Tel: 93.68.91.91

The first-floor dining-room and terrace of this new restaurant in the **Hotel Martinez** has a great view, subtle décor and fine cooking by Christian Willer.

LE ROYAL GRAY

6, rue des Etats-Unis.
Tel: 93.99.04.59

The formal dining room in the **Gray**

d'Albion hotel is a bit subdued but Jacques Chibois, who was trained by Michel Guérard and others, is one of the best 32-year-old chefs in France.

MOUGINS

LE RELAIS DE MOUGINS

Place de la Mairie
Tel: 93.90.03.47

André Surmain speaks the English of any chef on the *Côte* due to the many years he owned and ran **Lutèce** in New York. The main square of Mougins is quiet and his *menu gourmand* makes it great for corporate or other seductions.

NICE

LE CHANTECLER

37, Promenade des Anglais
Tel: 93.88.39.51

You'd think the **Hotel Negresco** could afford a dining room with a view, but it's worth putting up with the rooster-decorated walls if only to sample one of the best dessert menus in the world.

MONACO

LE GRILL DE L'HOTEL DE PARIS

Place du Casino
Tel: 93.50.80.80

At the top of the **Hôtel de Paris**, the view is better than the food, but it's a great place to entertain when there are fireworks.

RAMPOLDI

3, avenue des Spelugues
Tel: 93.30.70.65

The place to see Karl Lagerfeld and other hot personalities around town.

BUSINESS CONTACTS

COTE D'AZUR DEVELOPPEMENT

10, rue de la Préfecture
06300 NICE
Tel: 93.92.42.42
Telex: 470134F

The French Riviera Economic Development Agency – an important association whose members include businesses, universities, research institutes and local government bodies on the Riviera – informs foreign companies of the assets, policies, potential and problems of doing business on the Riviera. It is gradually becoming the one-stop umbrella organization for companies wishing to invest in or locate their operations in the South of France.

DELEGATION VALBONNE SOPHIA ANTIPOLIS

Place Joseph Bermond
06560 VALBONNE

Tel: 93.74.10.00
Telex: 461165F

This offshoot of the powerful Chamber of Commerce is responsible for the commercialization of the Sophia Antipolis technology park between Nice and Cannes, where 15O companies like IBM, Digital Equipment have offices.

DIRECTION DU TOURISME ET DES CONGRES DE LA PRINCIPAUTE DE MONACO
2a, boulevard des Moulins
Monte Carlo
MC 98030 MONACO
Tel: 93.30.87.01

They can help you set up a business or conference in one easy visit.

SYNDICAT DE L'INDUSTRIE DE L'HABILLEMENT DE LA COTE D'AZUR
2, boulevard Victor Hugo
06000 NICE
Tel: 93.88.79.51

Fashion information for professionals.

STUDIOS DE LA VICTORINE COTE D'AZUR
16, avenue Edouard Grinda
06200 NICE
Tel: 93.72.54.54.

The place to go if you want to shoot a film about it all.

BANKS

Most French and many international banks have offices in Cannes, Nice and Monaco.

AMERICAN EXPRESS
43, boulevard Albert Ier
ANTIBES
Tel: 93.34.74.56

2, rue du Congrès
06000 NICE
Tel: 93.87.11.76

8, rue des Belges
CANNES
Tel: 93.38.15.87

5, avenue de Monte Carlo
MONACO
Tel: 93.50.07.77

BANQUE NATIONALE DE PARIS
2, boulevard Victor-Hugo
06000 NICE
Tel: 93.88.39.31

BARCLAYS BANK
2, rue Alphonse-Karr
06000 NICE
Tel: 93.87.92.31

CHASE MANHATTAN BANK
27, avenue de la Costa
Monte Carlo
MC 98000 MONACO
Tel: 93.25.72.72

CITIBANK
2, avenue de Monte Carlo
MC 98003 MONACO
Tel: 93.50.96.06

CREDIT LYONNAIS
15, avenue Jean Médecin
06000 NICE
Tel: 93.82.83.33

GRINDLAYS BANK
1, rue Maréchal Joffre
06000 NICE
Tel: 93.87.43.52

INTERNATIONAL WESTMINSTER BANK
6, avenue de Verdun
06000 NICE
Tel: 93.88.88.66

LLOYDS BANK
14, rue Venizelos
06400 CANNES
Tel: 93.99.03.54.

BROKERS

BACHE SECURITIES
Sporting d'Hiver
Monte Carlo
MC 98000 MONACO
Tel: 93.50.71.71

MERRILL LYNCH S.A.M.
Les Terrasses
2, avenue de Monte Carlo
Monte Carlo
MC 98003 MONACO
Tel: 93.50.21.21

SHEARSON LEHMAN BROTHERS
5, Impasse Fontaine
Monte Carlo
MC 98003 MONACO
Tel: 93.25.01.00

CONSULATES

AMERICAN CONSULATE
9, rue Armeny
13006 MARSEILLE
Tel: 91.54.92.00

BRITISH CONSULATE
11, rue Paradis
06000 NICE
Tel: 93.82.32.04

CANADIAN CONSULATE
24, avenue du Prado
13006 MARSEILLE
Tel: 91.37.19.37

CONVENTIONS AND CONFERENCES

Most local communities have convention centers of varying sizes but Cannes, Nice and Monaco are favorite sites for the more prestigious gatherings.

ACROPOLIS
Palais des Congrès de Nice
Esplanade Kennedy
06058 NICE
Tel: 93.92.83.00

ANTIBES PALAIS DES CONGRES
Square Sydney Bechet
06160 JUAN-LES-PINS
Tel: 93.61.26.56

DIRECTION DU TOURISME ET DES CONGRES DE LA PRINCIPAUTE DE MONACO
2a, boulevard des Moulins
Monte Carlo
MC98030 MONACO
Tel: 93.30.87.01

PALAIS DES FESTIVALS ET DES CONGRES DE CANNES
Office du Tourisme de
la Ville de Cannes
Esplanade President Georges Pompidou
06400 CANNES
Tel: 93.39.01.01

VILLEFRANCHE SUR MER SERVICE DES CONGRES
Citadelle de Villefranche
06230
VILLEFRANCHE-SUR-MER
Tel: 93.55.45.12

LAWYERS

DONALD MANASSE
44, boulevard d'Italie
MC 98000 MONACO
Tel: 93.50.91.72

AVERY ELIZABETH GLIZE-KANE
20, boulevard de la République
06400 CANNES
Tel: 93.99.40.78

REAL-ESTATE AGENCIES

If it appears that there are as many real-estate agencies (there are 26 pages' worth in the yellow pages of the telephone directory) as bakeries in the South of France, you might get an idea where people think their bread is buttered. Among the best known for providing their clients with English speakers.

AGEDI
26 bis, boulevard Princesse Charlotte
MC 98000 MONACO
Tel: 93.50.66.00

JOHN TAYLOR
55, boulevard de la Croisette
06400 CANNES
Tel: 93.38.00.66

JOHN TAYLOR
1, avenue Gustave V
06000 NICE
Tel: 93.88.90.25

SSI
47, boulevard de la Croisette
06400 CANNES
Tel: 93.38.19.19

SERVICES

AIRPORT 2A SERVICE
"Welcome to the Côte d'Azur"
Tel: 93.21.30.73

Affiliate of *Chambre de Commerce et de l'Industrie*, they will make you feel at home with a welcome sign in front of the airport arrivals (300 F for one day) and provide a reception desk at your conference (1,000 F a day). In addition they can provide business services at the airport.

Office, Secretary, etc.

ACTE
Les Algorythmes
Sophia Antipolis
06560 VALBONNE
Tel: 93.65.38.00

BUSINESS AIDES ASSOCIATES
1, avenue Henry Dunant
MONACO
Tel: 93.50.2[illegible]

GRAPH'ECLAIR
61, avenue Henri Dunant
06000 NICE
Tel: 93.52.46.16

V.I.P. SERVICE INTERNATIONAL
P.O.B. 221
MONACO
Tel: 93.25.55.99

V.I.P. RIVIERA SERVICE
2O5, Promenade des Anglais 06200 NICE
Tel: 93.44.22.33

Airfreight

DHL INTERNATIONAL
SAINT LAURENT DU VAR
Tel: 93.07.75.28

Interpreters

MRS G.DE CRUZ SANTOS
Coaraze
06390 CONTES
Tel: 93.79.08.54

For multi-lingual interpreters and simultaneous interpretation into French, English, Spanish, German and Italian.

Chauffeur-Driven Cars

GARAGE PLAZA
NICE: 93.87.82.34
CANNES: 93.87.97.23

They pick you up and cater to your whims.

Joel Stratte-McClure

JOEL STRATTE-McCLURE is a freelance journalist, living in the South of France, who writes for many international publications. He also publishes "Sophialet", a newsletter about the Sophia Antipolis high technology area.

9
8

Le Maire de Nice

Nice, Summer 1986

Welcome to the French Riviera. Our land is a privileged one. It enjoys a worldwide reputation for tourism and *douceur de vivre,* but it also offers tremendous business assets.

The French Riviera means 300 days of sunshine per year, miles of beaches, Marinas, ski resorts, museums, art galleries, the biggest concentration in the world of convention centers.

But it is also 20 industrial and high technology estates, including Sophia-Antipolis, the largest Research and Science park in Europe.

It boasts the highest ratio of scientists per inhabitant in France, young universities in full expansion, and Research Centers.

Major American companies such as Digital Equipment, Dow Chemical, IBM, Rohm and Haas, Texas Instruments, G.D. Searle, Sperry, are taking advantage of the Riviera's productive climate, high technology environment and quality of life.

I am pleased to welcome you to my part of the world where you'll enjoy business and leisure activities in complete friendliness and safety.

Cordially yours,

Jacques Médecin,
Mayor of Nice
President of the Council for the French Riviera
Member of Parliament
Former Secretary of Tourism

My Touch of Monaco and the French Riviera

Monday a.m. Flea Market Cours Saleya
Cap 3000 Supermarket
Wednesday Artists Cours Saleya
Cimiez High Class Suburbs Hotels etc
Village Segurane Antique area Rue Catherine Segur
Les Puces Flea Market Boulevarde Risso
Alps Region Park National Du Mercantour
Wednesday Tour La Suisse Nicoise Les 3 Valleys

La Rotonde @ Negresco

My Touch of Monaco and the French Riviera

My Touch of Monaco and the French Riviera

My Touch of Monaco and the French Riviera

My Touch of Monaco and the French Riviera

Photocomposition : ITALIQUES
Photogravure : CENTRE SCANNER PHOTOGRAVURE (C.S.P.)
Impression : NORMANDIE IMPRESSION
Dépôt Légal : 2e trimestre 1986 1re édition

The information in this guide was accurate as of spring 1986, its publishing date. As prices, phone numbers and/or addresses may change without notice, there may be some discrepancies between our material and reality due to circumstances beyond our control; we hope this is a rare occurence.